MORE
COMMUNICATION KEYS FOR YOUR
MARRIAGE

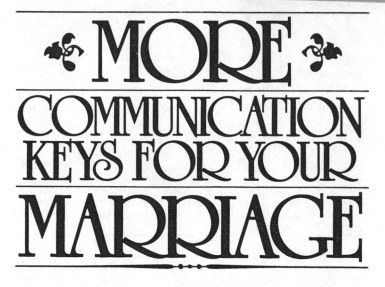

H. Norman Wright

Regal Books
A Division of GL Publications
Ventura, CA U.S.A.

Other Regal reading by H. Norman Wright
Communication: Key to Your Marriage
The Pillars of Marriage
Preparing for Parenthood
Seasons of a Marriage
So You're Getting Married

Rights for publishing this book in other languages are contracted by Gospel Literature International (GLINT) foundation. GLINT also provides technical help for the adaptation, translation and publishing of Bible study resources and books in scores of languages worldwide. For further information, contact GLINT, Post Office Box 6688, Ventura, California 93006, U.S.A., or the publisher.

Scripture quotations in this publication, unless otherwise indicated, are from the *New American Standard Bible*, Copyright © The Lockman Foundation 1960, 1962, 1963, 1968, 1971, 1972, 1973, 1975. Used by permission. Also quoted are:
AMP—The Amplified Bible. Copyright © 1962, 1964 by Zondervan Publishing House. Used by permission.
NIV—New International Version, Holy Bible. Copyright © 1973 and 1978 by New York International Bible Society. Used by permission.
RSV—Revised Standard Version of the Bible, copyrighted 1946 and 1952 by the Division of Christian Education of the NCCC, U.S.A. and used by permission.
TLB—The Living Bible, Copyright © 1971 by Tyndale House Publishers, Wheaton, Illinois. Used by permission.
KJV—Authorized King James Version.

Library of Congress Cataloging in Publication Data

Wright, H. Norman.
   More communication keys for your marriage.

   Includes bibliographical references.
   1. Communication in marriage.   2. Marriage—Religious aspects—Christianity.   I. Title.
HQ734.W9494   1983   646.7'8   83-11151
ISBN 0-8307-0904-5

3 4 5 6 7 8 9 10 11 12 / 91 90 89 88 87 86

CONTENTS

CHAPTER 1

WHAT MAKES A MARRIAGE?

Why did you marry? Can you remember back to that time when your life was filled with dreams, expectations, and hopes for the future? What part did marriage play in those dreams and hopes? How did you look at marriage? What did you expect from your marriage? Your answer might include one or more of the following:

"I wanted to share my life experiences with someone."

"I wanted someone to help make me happy."

"I wanted to spend my life with someone I loved and with someone who loved me."

"I didn't want to spend my life alone."

"I wanted to fulfill what I lacked in my own home."

"I wanted to be faithful to God and love someone He wanted me to love."

"I didn't want to end up alone, especially when I was older. Marriage was that security."

"I wanted the security of a permanent relationship."

All of these are fringe benefits of marriage, but none is strong enough to stand as a foundation for marriage.

Many people are propelled toward marriage without really understanding all they are committing themselves to for the rest of their lives. That is why couples experience surprises and upsets through the duration of their marriage. Marriage is many things:

Marriage is a gift.

Marriage is an opportunity for love to be learned.

Marriage is a journey in which we as the travelers are faced with many choices and we are responsible for these choices.

Marriage is affected more by our inner communication than our outer communication.

Marriage is more often influenced by unresolved issues from our past than we realize.

Marriage is a call to servanthood.

Marriage is a call to friendship.

Marriage is a call to suffering.

Marriage is a refining process. It is an opportunity to be refined by God into the person He wants us to be.

Marriage is not an event but a way of life.

Marriage involves intimacy in all areas for it to be fulfilling. This intimacy must reach into the spiritual, the intellectual, the social, the emotional, and the physical.

I have selected four of these beliefs for you to consider in this chapter. Think about each of these as you reflect on your own marriage relationship. What you believe about marriage and what you expect out of your marriage has a direct effect on communication between you and your spouse.

I believe that (1) marriage is a gift, (2) marriage is a call to servanthood, (3)marriage involves intimacy, and (4) marriage is a refining process.

MARRIAGE IS A GIFT

Marriage is a gift. *You* may be the finest gift your spouse has ever received! Your spouse may be the finest gift you have received.

A gift is an item which is selected with care and consideration. Its purpose is to bring delight and fulfillment to another, an expression of deep feeling on the part of the giver. Think of the care and effort you put into selecting a gift.

You wonder what the recipient would enjoy. What will bring him/her delight? What will bring happiness?

What will make his/her day bright and cheery? What will show the person the extent of your feeling for him/her and how much the person means to you?

Because you want this gift to be special and meaningful you spend time thinking about what gift to select. Then you begin the search through various stores and shops, considering and rejecting several items until the right one beckons to you and you make the selection. You invest time wrapping the gift. You think of how best to present it to the person so his/her delight and pleasure will be heightened.

There is an excitement and a challenge involved in selecting and presenting a special gift. You not only have given the object, you also have given your time and energy. Gifts which are often appreciated the most are not those which are the most expensive, but are those which reflect the investment of yourself in considering the desires and wants of the other person, and the way you present it and the sacrifice you make.

You are a gift to your spouse. If you consider that you are a gift, how do you live so that your spouse feels that he/she has been given a special gift? Do you invest your time, thought, and energy to your spouse? Does your spouse experience delight, fulfillment, and a feeling of being special? How can you, as a gift, be used in the life of your spouse to lift his/her spirits and out-look on life?

On the receiving end of the gift, how do you react when you receive a special gift which brings you delight? Think of your childhood or earlier years. What was the most exciting or special gift you ever received? Can you remember your thoughts and feelings as you received that gift? How did you treat that gift? Did you take special care of it and protect it from harm and loss? Perhaps you gave the gift a special place of prominence and were carefully possessive of it.

If your spouse is a special gift to you, how do you treat this gift? Are you careful to give your spouse the finest care, attention, protection and place of prominence in your life? Does your partner feel as though he/she really is a gift to you?

A gift is given as an expression of our love. It is not based on whether the recipient deserves it or not. Our giving of a gift is actually an act of grace.

What Do You Think?

1. What is the best tangible gift your spouse has ever given you?

2. What is the best intangible gift your spouse has ever given you?

3. What is the gift you would like to give to your spouse?

4. What would your spouse appreciate?

MARRIAGE IS SERVANTHOOD

Marriage is a call to servanthood. This is not a very popular concept and not high on the list of priorities for most marriages. We would much rather be served than to serve. But our guideline for a Christian marriage is given to us from the Scriptures. Look at the following passages:

"Do not merely look out for your own personal interests, but also for the interests of others. Have this attitude in yourselves which was also in Christ Jesus, who, although He existed in the form of God, did not regard equality with God a thing to be grasped, but emptied Himself, taking the form of a bond-servant, and being made in the likeness of men. And being found in appearance as a man, He humbled Himself by becoming obedient to the point of death, even death on a cross. Therefore also God highly exalted Him, and bestowed on Him the name which is above every name" (Phil. 2:4-9). Jesus voluntarily submitted to becoming a "bond-servant," looking out for our interests rather than His own. In the same way the Apostle Paul tells us to "be subject to one another in the fear of Christ" (Eph. 5:21).

Notice one important point: We must never *demand* that our partner be our servant or live up to the clear teachings of Scripture. If we feel that we have to demand it, or even to mention it, then we become more concerned with meeting our own needs than with being a servant. If a man has to demand that his wife see him as the head of the family, then—to be blunt—he has lost it! Verses 22-25 say that for a man to be the head he must love his wife as Christ loved the church and gave Himself for her. This means sacrificial love—servanthood.

The Greek word translated "submit" in Ephesians 5:21 is *hupotasso*. It is also translated "subject" and is used several times in the New Testament. The active form of this verb is a military term. It signifies an externally imposed submission based upon someone's rank or position, such as a private or sergeant would submit to a captain or lieutenant. In Scripture the word emphasizes the rule of Jesus Christ, such as in Romans 8:20 when speaking of "the creation" being subject to Christ. Again, in 1 Corinthians 15:27, on three occasions God is said to have put all things under Jesus' feet, making them subject to Him. This is *hupotasso* in the active voice.

However, the word *hupotasso* has another form, the middle or passive voice. Here subjection is not something which is arbitrarily done to you, but is something you do voluntarily to yourself. In the various marriage texts such as Colossians 3, Ephesians 5, Titus 2, and 1 Peter 3, the word *hupotasso* is in the middle or passive voice. The submission you are called to in marriage is never anything which is externally imposed, but is a definite act on your part which comes from inside you. And it is a mutual submission, not one way.

A great deal has been said in recent years about the husband/wife relationship as described in Scripture. With the feminist movement demanding that women be treated as equals, the Bible scholars have struggled with the true meaning of passages such as Ephesians 5. Some have incorrectly interpreted the word submit in the "military" sense of the word, proclaiming the absolute headship of the husband. Others have swung the other way saying that husbands and wives are equal, and the only kind of marriage that is biblical is one of an equal partnership. As often happens, we struggle with one of many paradoxes in Scripture.

I think perhaps Dwight Small best describes the biblical roles of husbands and wives in his book *Marriage as Equal Partnership*. He states:

> It is good that husband-wife equality is a prominent concern in our time. We are whole-heartedly in favor of extending that equality to every facet of daily living. But there is one thing we must remember. Equality is one principle among others; it doesn't stand alone and unqualified as though it were the only word of God to us. It is only part of the divine equation. It is entirely true, it is not the entire truth. And what humanly seems contradictory to us may be a divine paradox. Thus, in Ephesians 5:21-33 it becomes obvious that husbands and wives are equal in every respect save one—authority and responsibility.
>
> As we've begun to see, this inequality in authority-responsibility is mitigated inasmuch as the husband carries this as his own peculiar burden before the Lord. It is not to be envied, only supported prayerfully. What truly does alleviate all wifely fears is the call to mutual love and Christlike service at the heart of this paradoxical relationship. Its beauty, symmetry, and fairness unfold as we place ourselves within these special conditions under which biblical marriage functions.
>
> Headship is not at all a husband's becoming a master, boss, tyrant, authoritarian—the dominant

IF A MAN HAS TO DEMAND THAT HIS WIFE SEE HIM AS HEAD OF THE FAMILY, HE'S HAD IT!

coercive force. Neither does it imply control or restriction, his being assertive and hers being suppressed. It cannot mean he assumes any prerogatives of greater virtue, intelligence, or ability. It does not mean that he is active and she passive, he the voice and she the silent partner. Nor does it mean that he is the tribal chief, the family manager, the one who has superior rights or privileges. He is not the decision-maker, problem-solver, goal-setter, or director of everyone else in the family's life. Rather he is primarily responsible for their common advance toward freedom and fellowship—creating a partnership of equals under one responsible head.

A truly loving husband will regard his wife as a completely equal partner in everything that concerns their life together. He will assert his headship to see that this equal partnership is kept inviolable. Hers is to be an equal contribution in areas, say, of decision-making, conflict-resolution, emerging family developmental planning, and daily family management. Whether it concerns finances, or child discipline, or social life—whatever it may be, she is an equal partner. Loving headship affirms, defers, shares; it encourages and stimulates. Loving headship delights to delegate without demanding. Yet, throughout the equalitarian process, the husband knows all the while that he bears the responsibility before God for the healthful maintenance of the marriage.[1]

We are on the safe side when we see the definition of subjection in the person of Jesus Himself. He, being free, abased Himself for us. He, being equal with the Father, relinquished that equality to become the Servant for all of us. Subjection, then, means no less than adopting His way of self-denial for the sake of others . . . .

Every Christian is called to servanthood as the expression of his or her new life in Christ. This is emphasized in Paul's reference to Jesus' taking the form of a servant: "Have this mind among your-selves . . . " (Phil. 2:5). Servanthood is the identify-ing mark of every true Christian believer.[2]

To put it simply, a servant's role is to make sure that the other person's needs are met. In a husband-wife relationship, being a servant is an act of love, a gift to the other person to make his/her life fuller. It is not something to be demanded. It is an act of strength and not of weakness. It is a positive action which has been chosen to show your love to each another. Hence, the apostle also said, "Be subject to one another," not limiting the role of servanthood to the wife.

A servant may also be called an *enabler*. The word *enable* means "to make better." As an enabler we are to make life eas-ier for our spouse instead of placing restrictive demands upon him/her. An enabler does not make more work for the partner, nor does he/she hinder the other from becoming all he/she has been designed to become.

A servant is also one who *edifies* or builds up the other per-son. The English word *edify* is derived from the Latin word *aedes* meaning "hearth" or "fireplace." The hearth was the center of activity in ancient times. It was the only place of warmth and light in the home, and the place where the daily bread was pre-pared. It was also the place where people were drawn together.

Edifying is often used in the New Testament to refer to building up another person. Three examples of edifying are expressed in the verses below: (1) personal encouragement, (2) inner strengthening, and (3) the establishment of peace and har-mony between individuals.

"So let us then definitely aim for and eagerly pursue what makes for harmony and for mutual upbuilding (edificiation and development) of one another" (Rom. 14:19, *AMP*).

"Let each one of us make it a practice to please (make happy) his neighbor for his good and for his true welfare, to edify him—that is, to strengthen him and build him up spiritually" (Rom. 15:2, *AMP*).

"Therefore encourage one another and build each other up,

just as in fact you are doing" (1 Thess. 5:11, *NIV*).

First Corinthians 8:1 sums up the matter of edifying: "Love builds up" *(NIV)*.

To *edify* then, means to cheer another person on in life. You are a one-person rooting section for your spouse which can increase your spouse's feelings of self-worth. The result is that your spouse's capacity to love and give in return is enhanced.

Elizabeth Barrett Browning described the essence of edifying when she wrote to the man she would marry, "Make thy love larger to enlarge my worth."

To encourage your spouse is to inspire him or her with renewed courage, spirit, and hope. It is an act of affirmation for who the person is.

MARRIAGE INVOLVES INTIMACY

Marriage is a way of life, a celebration of life. A wedding ends but a marriage progresses until the death of one of the partners. The conclusion of the wedding marks the beginning of a marriage relationship which is a call to intimacy. Intimacy is shared identity, a "we" relationship. Its opposite is a marriage in which the individuals are called "married singles"—each partner goes his own way. In shared intimacy there must be a level of honesty which makes each vulnerable to the other. Intimacy is like a multi-stringed musical instrument. The music which comes from a viola comes not from one string but from a combination of different strings and finger positions.

We hear a great deal today about physical intimacy, often referring to nothing more than the physical act of two bodies copulating. However, the basis for true physical intimacy actually results from two other critical areas—*emotional intimacy* and *aesthetic intimacy.*

A physical marriage involves the *marriage of emotions* as well as bodies. Emotions give color to life. Emotional intimacy eludes many couples because one or both make no conscious effort to develop its potential. A man's and woman's emotions may be at different levels and intensities, or a woman's priority may be emotional intimacy whereas the man's priority is physical. When a couple learns to share the emotional level, when they can understand and experience each other's feelings, they are well on the way to achieving true intimacy. Barriers and walls must be lowered for intimacy to develop.

Judson Swihart writes of the tragedy of a marriage lacking emotional intimacy. "Some people are like medieval castles. Their high walls keep them safe from being hurt. They protect themselves emotionally by permitting no exchange of feelings with others. No one can enter. They are secure from attack. However, inspection of the occupant finds him or her lonely, rattling around his castle alone. The castle dweller is a self-made prisoner. He or she needs to feel loved by someone, but the walls are so high that it is difficult to reach out or for anyone else to reach in."[3]

The poem "Walls" describes the devastations of this barrier.

> Their wedding picture mocked them from the table,
>   these two
>   whose minds no longer touched each other.
> They lived with such a heavy barricade between
>   them that
>   neither battering ram of words nor artilleries of
>   touch
>   could break it down.
> Somewhere, between the oldest child's first tooth
>   and the
>   youngest daughter's graduation, they lost each
>   other.
> Throughout the years, each slowly unraveled that
>   tangled ball
>   of string called self, and as they tugged at stub-
>   born
>   knots each hid his searching from the other.
> Sometimes she cried at night and begged the whis-
>   pering dark-
>   ness to tell her who she was.
> He lay beside her, snoring like a hibernating bear,
>   unaware
>   of her winter.

Once, after they had made love, he wanted to tell her how
afraid he was of dying, but fearing to show his naked
soul, he spoke instead about the beauty of her breasts.
She took a course in modern art, trying to find herself in
colors splashed upon a canvas, and complaining to other
women about men who were insensitive.
He climbed a tomb called "the office," wrapped his mind in
a shroud of paper figures and buried himself in customers.
Slowly, the wall between them rose, cemented by the mortar
of indifference.
One day, reaching out to touch each other, they found a barrier
they could not penetrate, and recoiling from the coldness
of the stone, each retreated from the stranger on the
other side.
For when love dies, it is not in a moment of angry battle,
nor when fiery bodies lose their heat.
It lies panting, exhausted, expiring at the bottom of a wall
it could not scale.[4]

Another form of intimacy is *aesthetic intimacy*, sharing the experiences of beauty. One couple enjoys sharing music, while another may prefer an oil painting of a mountain scene. Have you discovered this area of intimacy in your marriage yet? Careful and thoughtful questioning, or listening with your eyes may help you make this discovery.

To me one of the most beautiful and restful places on earth is found at the inlet of Jenny Lake in the Grand Tetons National Park. Following a trail along a rushing stream you stroll through woods for several hundred yards. Then you make a sudden hike down a slight hill to discover the inlet and the startling beauty of water, forest, sky, and jagged peaks. I value this place because of its beauty, isolation, and quietness. I have been there early in the morning on a clear, cloudless day, watching the sun creep slowly down the mountainside into the forest, and then brilliantly reflect off the smooth surface of the water.

At other times black clouds frame the rugged horizon and streaks of lightning provide a natural spectacle. I have sat upon a large boulder in a rainstorm with hailstones bouncing off my wide-brimmed hat as I pulled my coat tighter about me for protection. Each occasion provided a different kind of beauty, an experience that added to my reservoir of memories and built my anticipation of the next time. I have enjoyed this special place both by myself and with my wife Joyce.

Sharing and intimacy do not have to come from a series of comments like, "Isn't this beautiful?" or "Look at that!" or "Have you ever seen anything like this before?" Intimacy is standing together quietly, drinking in the amazing panorama and sensing the other's presence and appreciation. Beauty can be shared without a word. Such moments of sharing will be remembered for years and can be referred to again and again in private thought or in conversation.

Intimacy has been described as "we" experiences, a shared identity. In some marriages this "we" relationship does not develop and the result is a parallel marriage. The two individuals think mostly of themselves with little regard for the desires, wishes, or needs of their spouse.

For emotional and aesthetic intimacy to occur there must be communication. And for true communication to occur there must be emotional intimacy. Isn't this a paradox? Where do you begin?

Spiritual intimacy is another basis for true intimacy to occur. As a couple learns to communicate with each other and with God, they learn to trust each other and be more open. Spiritual intimacy comes from developing communication between ourselves and God in the presence of our spouse. It's easy to talk about, but not always easy to achieve.

What Do You Think?

1. What barrier to intimacy needs to be removed in your marriage?

2. Indicate a special time of intimacy you have experienced in the last month.

3. What could you do this week to increase the intimacy in your relationship?

MARRIAGE IS A REFINING PROCESS

Joyce and I married at the age of twenty-two, about twenty-four years ago. Much has occurred during these years. A discovery which came early in marriage was the awareness that marriage is a refining process. Two individuals living in such close proximity are going to have to mature and have their rough edges smoothed, or their faults will become intensified and enlarged, and their negative qualities more pronounced.

Daily there are opportunities for growth if we allow it to occur. We encounter both major and minor crises often, some predictable and some like alien invaders from outer space.

What causes a major crisis to become a restrictive, crippling, eternal tragedy rather than a growth-producing experience in spite of the pain?

Our attitude.

Crises and trials can become the means of exciting growth. In the book *Run from the Pale Pony,* William Pruitt uses an analogy to share what has happened in his life. In the foreword of the book he writes:

About thirty years ago, one of my joys as a boy was to ride a white horse named Prince. That proud, spirited stallion carried me where I wanted to go, wherever I bid him to and at the pace which I chose. I don't have to explain to horsemen the feeling of strength, even authority, which comes from controlling such a powerful animal. Nor need I expand upon the excitement I felt when I galloped him at full speed, or about the quiet pride that came when I twisted him through the corkscrew turns of a rodeo exercise. After all, he was mine and I trained him. Those experiences are part of my heritage.

My cherished white horse was gone and seldom remembered about fifteen years later. It was then that I encountered a completely different kind of horse. When I first became aware of the specter, its shape was too dim to discern. I know only that I had never seen anything like it before. Too, I know that I had not sought any such creature, yet something different was with me wherever I went and that shadow would not go away. I told myself, "Really, now, you're much too busy to bother with something that seems determined to disturb you, get rid of it." And I tried to will it away. No matter what I did though, the specter followed my every move. Furthermore, the harder I tried to lose it, the clearer the creature's form became to me.

My uneasiness changed to anxiety when I realized that this unwanted shadow had a will of its own. The chill of fear came when I understood that it had no intention to leave me alone. Without further warning, it began to communicate with me openly one day, and in a harsh voice which was almost rigid with animosity, it spat out, "You can no longer go where you want to go when you choose at the speed you pick. That's true because I will give you weakness instead of strength. Excitement and pride?

Never again will you have them like before. I plan only confinement and disability for you. And I will be your constant companion. My name is Chronic Illness."

At the time I heard it speak, I shrank back from actually seeing it face to face. It spoke harshly of miseries which were inverse to joys with my white horse named Health and the bitter irony was reflected in the form of a malicious creature. Chronic Illness took the shape of a stunted misshapen pony. Its shaggy coat was pale in color, streaked with ages old accumulation of dark despair. But, unquestionably, the most frightening feature of the animal was its overwhelming glare—its glare-eyed stare which held me helpless. The pony's wild eyes started restlessly from side to side, yet strangely were unblinding. This book is written first of all for those people who have met the pale pony face to face.[5]

There are many possible forms in which the "pale pony" might come—serious physical or mental illness, accident, war injuries, etc. Whatever shape the pony takes, the results can be quite similar. William Pruitt's pale pony was multiple sclerosis. He sensed that the disease was increasingly affecting his life, but his story is the story of hope. He realized that he had a number of years before he would be completely disabled, and realizing that he wouldn't be able to carry on the type of work he was in, he went back to college in a wheelchair. He earned a Ph.D. in economics and began to teach on the college level.

Pruitt's book is not a book about giving up but rather about fighting back and winning. It's a very honest book, telling of the pain and the hurt and the turmoil. But its emphasis is on faith and hope.

The key issue to life's crises is our response. When trouble comes can we honestly say, "God, this isn't what I wanted in my life, I didn't plan for this." But the trouble is there, regardless of our wishes. How will we respond to it?

A verse that has meant so much to me is one which I ask

couples in premarital counseling to build their marriage upon: "Consider it all joy, my brethren, when you encounter various trials, knowing that the testing [or trying] of your faith produces endurance" (Jas. 1:2-3). It's easy to read a passage like this and say, "Well, that's fine." It is another thing, however, to put it into practice.

What does the word *consider,* or *count,* actually mean? It refers to an internal attitude of the heart or the mind that allows the trial and circumstance of life to affect us adversely or beneficially. Another way James 1:2 might be translated is: "Make up your mind to regard adversity as something to welcome or be glad about."

You have the power to decide what your attitude will be. You can approach it and say: "That's terrible. Totally upsetting. That is the last thing I wanted for my life. Why did it have to happen now? Why me?"

The other way of "considering" the same difficulty is to say: "It's not what I wanted or expected, but it's here. There are going to be some difficult times, but how can I make the best of them?" Don't ever deny the pain or the hurt that you might have to go through, but always ask, "What can I learn from it, and how can it be used for God's glory?"

The verb tense used in the word *consider* indicates a decisiveness of action. It's not an attitude of resignation—"Well, I'll just give up. I'm just stuck with this problem. That's the way life is." If you resign yourself, you will sit back and not put forth any effort. The verb tense actually indicates that you will have to go against your natural inclination to see the trial as a negative force. There will be some moments when you won't see it like that at all, and then you'll have to remind yourself: "No, I think there is a better way of responding to this. Lord, I really want you to help me see it from a different perspective." And then your mind will shift to a more constructive response. This often takes a lot of work on your part.

God created us with both the capacity and the freedom to determine how we will respond to those unexpected incidents that life brings our way. You may honestly wish that a certain event had never occurred. But you cannot change the fact.

My wife, Joyce, and I have had to learn to look to God in the midst of a seeming tragedy. We have two children; a daughter, Sheryl, who is now twenty-two and a son, Matthew, who is sixteen. Mentally, however, Matthew is at less than a two-year-old level. He is a brain-damaged, mentally retarded boy who may never develop past the mental level of a three-year-old. Matthew can walk but he cannot talk or feed himself; he is not toilet trained. He is classified as profoundly retarded.

We did not anticipate becoming the parents of a mentally retarded son. We married upon graduation from college, proceeded through seminary and graduate school training, and into a local church ministry. Several years later, Matthew was born. We have learned and grown through the process of caring for him. As I look at my life, I know that I have been an impatient, selfish person in many ways. But because of Matthew, I had the opportunity to develop patience. When you wait for a long time for a child to be able to reach out and handle an item, when you wait for three or four years for him to learn to walk, you develop patience. We have had to learn to be sensitive to a person who cannot verbally communicate his needs, hurts, or wants. We must decipher what he is trying to say; we must try to interpret his nonverbal behavior.

Needless to say, Joyce and I have grown and changed through this process. We have experienced times of hurt, frustration, and sorrow. But we have rejoiced and learned to thank God for tiny steps of progress which most people would take completely for granted. The meaning of the name *Matthew*— "God's Gift" or "Gift from God"—has become very real to us.

We might very easily have chosen bitterness over our son's problem. We could have let it become a source of estrangement in our marriage, hindering our growth as individuals. But God enabled us to select the path of acceptance. We have grown and matured. Together. Not instantly, but over the course of several years. There have been steep places to overcome. But there have also been highlights and rich moments of reflection and delight. Matthew has become the refining agent that God is using to change us.

My wife and I discovered a great deal about the way God

works. We realized that He had prepared us years before for Matthew's coming, though we hadn't realized the preparation was taking place. When I was in seminary I was required to write a thesis. Not knowing what to write about, I asked one of my professors to suggest a topic. She assigned me the title, "The Christian Education of the Mentally Retarded Child." I knew absolutely nothing on the subject. But I learned in a hurry. I read books, went to classes, observed training sessions in hospitals and homes, and finally wrote the thesis. I rewrote it three times and my wife typed it three times before it was accepted.

Later on, my graduate studies in psychology required several hundred hours of internship in a school district. The school district assigned me the task of testing mentally retarded children and placing them in their respective classes.

While serving as minister of education in a church for six years, I was asked by the church board to develop a Sunday School program for retarded children. My duties included developing the ministry and the curriculum, and training the teachers.

Two years before Matthew was born, Joyce and I were talking one evening. One of us said, "Isn't it interesting that we have all this exposure to retarded children? We've been learning so much. Could it be that God is preparing us for something that is going to occur later on in our life?" That's all we said at the time. I can't even remember which one of us said it. Within a year, Matthew was born. Eight months after that his seizures began. The uncertainty we had felt over the rate of his progress was now a deep concern. Then we learned the full truth and we began to see how the Lord had prepared us.

Where does the call to suffering enter into this whole process? Romans 8:16-17 says, "The Spirit Himself bears witness with our spirit that we are children of God, and if children, heirs also, heirs of God and fellow-heirs with Christ, if indeed we suffer with Him in order that we may also be glorified with Him." As members of the Body of Christ, we suffer when one member suffers.

In the minor or major crises which will occur in your marriage each person will experience hurt. Hurt shared, diminishes; carried alone it expands. Lewis B. Smedes describes marital suffering in this way. "Anybody's marriage is a harvest of suffering. Romantic lotus-eaters may tell you marriage was designed to be a pleasure-dome for erotic spirits to frolic in self-fulfilling relations. But they play you false. Your marriage vow was a promise to suffer. Yes, to suffer; I will not take it back. You promised to suffer with. It made sense, because the person you married was likely to get hurt he or she was bound to get. And you promised to hurt with your spouse. A marriage is a life of shared pain."[6]

This is a privilege! This is our ministry to one another! This is a reflection of the gift of marriage! How will you respond to this aspect of marriage?

Notes

1. Dwight H. Small, *Marriage as Equal Partnership* (Grand Rapids: Baker Book House, 1980.) pp. 29,30,48.
2. Ibid., p. 63.
3. Judson Swihart, *How Do I Say I Love You?* (Downers Grove, IL: InterVarsity Press, 1977), pp. 46-47.
4. Source unknown.
5. William Pruitt, *Run from the Pale Pony* (Grand Rapids: Baker Book House, 1976), pp. 9-10.
6. Lewis B. Smedes, *How Can It Be All Right When Everything Is All Wrong?* (San Francisco: Harper & Row, 1982), p. 61.

CHAPTER 2

YOUR INNER CONVERSATIONS

Each of us carries on conversations with ourselves daily. This doesn't mean that we are odd or on the verge of spacing out. It's normal to talk to oneself. After you complete this chapter, however, I hope you will be much more conscious of your self talk. You will probably be shocked by the amount of time you spend on inner conversations and how those conversations affect your marriage.

Are you aware that:

- most of your emotions—such as anger, depression, guilt, worry—are initiated and escalated by your self talk?
- the way you behave toward your spouse is determined by your self talk and not by his or her behavior?

- what you say and how you say it is a direct expression of your self talk?

Self talk is the message you tell yourself—the words you tell yourself about yourself, your spouse, your experiences, the past, the future, God, etc. It is a set of evaluating thoughts about facts and events that happen to you. As events are repeated, many of your thoughts, and thus your emotional responses, become almost automatic. Sometimes the words you tell yourself are never put together in clear statements. They may be more like impressions.

Self talk or inner conversation is not an emotion or feeling. It is also not an attitude. However, repeated sets of self talk *become* attitudes, values, and beliefs. Attitudes are with us for a long period of time and may be inactive. Self talk represents the evaluating thoughts that we give ourselves at the present time. Your expressions of anger, ways of showing love, how you handle conflict, are motivated by conscious and subconscious self talk. Your self talk may be based upon some of your attitudes. A positive attitude toward life would tend to generate positive self talk and a negative attitude, negative self talk. Self talk is different from our beliefs, yet it is often *based* on our beliefs.

Most people believe that outside events, other people, and circumstances determine their emotions, behaviors, and verbal responses. Actually, however, your thoughts are the source. What you think about these things and about people will determine the emotions you feel and the behaviors and verbal responses you express.

As an example of *your beliefs* affecting your self talk, consider these typical beliefs about marriage:

1. A spouse should make me happy.
2. A spouse should meet all of my needs.
3. A spouse should know what my needs are without having to tell him/her.
4. A spouse should be willing to do things according to my way of doing them.
5. A spouse should not respond in an irritable or angry way to me.

What Do You Think?

Assume that none of the above beliefs were true in your marriage. What do you think you would be saying to yourself? Write out your response for each one.

1.

2.

3.

4.

5.

Another example of the results of self talk can be seen in two different groups of people: those with a failure identity and those with a success identity. Each identity appears to be tied into the person's self talk. Positive self talk statements would include the following: "I have value and worth as a person"; "I have accomplished much of what I have tried in the past"; "Trying a new venture is worthwhile"; "If something is new, I see it as a challenge and an opportunity for me to grow."

A failure identity can come from statements like "I'm not as capable as others"; "I will probably fail"; "I can't accomplish what I try"; "If I try I might fail and others will see my weaknesses."

Let's consider for a moment this exchange between a husband and wife and discover the self talk that prompted it.

Saturday morning, 11:00 A.M.

Wife It's about time you got up. It looks like you're going to waste the entire day!

Husband (looking a bit startled) What's with you? I'm just taking my time getting up and enjoying a day off.

    Wife That's just it. You're around here so rarely and half the day is shot! By the time you get dressed and cleaned up lunch will be over and nothing has been accomplished!

Husband Who said I was getting dressed and cleaned up? The only thing I want to accomplish is a cup of coffee, the paper and the football game on TV!

    Wife What? Then the whole day is shot to . . . I don't get a day off. There's a whole list of work to be done here. When *are* you going to do it?

Husband What? I suppose you've been saving up a list of work projects again. Why don't you give me some notice ahead of time? If I wanted to work today, I could go into the shop and get overtime plus some peace and quiet!

What is happening in this conversation? First of all, each person has an unspoken expectation for Saturday. One for work and one for pleasure. Many problems such as this could be eliminated if individuals clarified their expectations in advance. Let's look at the wife's self talk at this point. She was expecting her husband to accomplish a number of tasks on Saturday. She got up at 6:30. Note her inner conversation and the progression.

   7:30 "I hope he gets up pretty soon. I'd like to get started on these projects. With the kids away today we can get a lot done."

   8:15 "Boy! I don't hear a sound. Well, I'm going to start work in the yard. He'll probably hear me and then he can join me."

   9:15 "What time is it? 9:15! I don't believe it! He's sleeping away the morning. Who does he think he is? How thoughtless! I ought to go in there and wake him up!"

  10:00 "Just because he has no work at the plant or at church he thinks he's entitled to sack out. What about me? When do I ever get to do this? He ticks me off! He probably knows I want him to take care of those chores he's been putting off. He just wants to ignore them and me! Boy, is he going to hear from me. I'll let him sleep but he's going to pay a price for it!"

10:45 "And I was going to cook his favorite meal and dessert tonight. Fat chance of that. How could he be so insensitive? Look at all I do for him!"

What type of emotions do these statements arouse? What kind of behaviors do you think these statements prompt? What kind of communication is happening?

Suppose, instead, the wife chose self talk such as the following:

"I wish he would get up. I think I'll check and see if he's just resting or sleeping."

"I'm not sure he's going to get up in time to do much today. I'd better revise my list and then ask him if he could help me with these two chores after lunch."

"I am a bit upset with him but I have to admit I didn't tell him I wanted him to work today. Next time I'll talk it over with him before the weekend."

"I could serve him breakfast in bed when he wakes up. That'll knock his socks off! When's the last time I did that?"

Two different styles of self talk. The choice is ours whether to make our self talk positive or negative.

Many of your thoughts are automatic. You don't sit around thinking about what you are going to think next. Thoughts slide into our consciousness so smoothly that you don't even sense their entrance. Many of them are stimulated from past experience, attitudes and beliefs. You build up storehouses of memories and experience, retaining and remembering those things which you concentrate upon the most.

Whether they are automatic or consciously thought out, what are your thoughts like? Are they negative or positive? Most people who worry, are depressed, irritable, or are critical toward others have automatic thoughts which are negative.

A characteristic of negative thoughts is that they are generally wrong. They do not reflect reality. Often they reflect our insecurity, our feelings of inadequacy, and our fears. These alien invaders are not usually welcome guests. They are generally exaggerated negative conclusions about our future, our spouse, our marriage, our everyday life, and ourselves.

What Do You Think?

If you have negative thoughts, and give into them without countering and evaluating them, the results will be negative. Consider the examples of thinking errors listed below which we either consciously conjure up or which jump into our mind. As you read each one, indicate in the space provided whether you have this type of thought. Then write an example of your most recent one. Try to remember what you said to your spouse based upon your thoughts.

Personalizing—Thinking that all situations and events revolve around you. "Everyone at my spouse's business party thought I looked out of place."

Example:

What I said:

Magnifying—Blowing negative events out of proportion. "This is the worst thing that could have happened to me."

Example:

What I said:

Minimizing—Glossing over the positive factors. Overlooking the fact that everything went well such as hosting a successful dinner. This could include explaining away or discounting a compliment.

Example:

What I said:

Either/or thinking. "Either I'm a successful spouse or a total failure."
Example:

What I said:

Taking events out of context—After a delightful day with your spouse, focusing on one or two rough spots. "The day was really a loss because of . . . "
Example:

What I said:

Jumping to conclusions. "My spouse isn't paying me as much attention. His/her love for me is fading."
Example:

What I said:

Over-generalizing. "I never can please him/her. I constantly blow it as a married partner." Or "He/she can never do anything right. He/she will always be this way."

Example:

What I said:

Self blame—Blaming the total self rather than specific behaviors that can be changed. "I'm no good as a marriage partner."
Example:

What I said:

Magical. "My marriage is all messed up because of my lousy past."
Example:

What I said:

Mind reading. "My spouse thinks I'm unattractive and fat."
Example:

What I said:

Comparing—"Comparing yourself with someone else and ignor-

ing all of the basic differences between the two of you. "My husband is much smarter than I am."
Example:

What I said:

Here are some examples of a few of these statements and how to counter them.

> *Wife:* "I'll never be able to satisfy my husband. I've made too many mistakes these first three years of marriage."
>
> *Thinking Error:* *Over-generalization*
>
> *Response:* "I don't know that I won't be able to satisfy him. I can grow and develop as a person. I can change. Where's the evidence that I'll *never* be able to? Here is what I will attempt today—"

> *Husband:* "My work isn't exciting or challenging at all. My life isn't fulfilling anymore."
>
> *Thinking Error:* *Minimizing* (disqualifying the positive)
>
> *Response:* "My work may not be exciting but there is a purpose to it. Have I focused on that? Have I thought of how this job affects others? Just because my work is not challenging, who says the rest of my life can't be fulfilling? What can I do at this time to enrich my life?"

> *Wife:* "I'll probably mess up this new recipe. Then my husband will get angry at me and won't speak to me the rest of the evening."
>
> *Thinking Error:* *Jumping to conclusions*
>
> *Response:* "I don't have to be a perfect cook. I can make it better the next time if it doesn't turn out

COUNTERING AUTOMATIC
THOUGHTS IS BRINGING
YOUR THOUGHTS TO TRIAL
AND EXAMINING THE
EVIDENCE.

too well. If he becomes angry, I can let him know that I'm disappointed too, but it's not the end of the world."

Husband: "What's the point in doing that for her? She wouldn't like it or she probably won't even notice it."
Thinking Error: *Mind reading*
Response: "I have no way of knowing. I can at least try. I need to give her a chance to respond. I might be surprised. If she doesn't care, it's not the end of the world."[1]

HOW TO CONTROL YOUR THOUGHTS

There are several basic ways of controlling your automatic thoughts and giving yourself an opportunity to produce more positive communication. The first is to become aware of these thoughts by keeping track of them. Writing them on a piece of paper or 3 x 5 card is one way to accomplish this.

Another way to eliminate automatic thoughts is to learn to counter or answer them. Countering is bringing your thoughts to trial and examining the evidence. But you can do this only if you are aware of them. You need to catch the thoughts that come into your mind, and then, when you are aware of them, respond with a conscious thought. You need not settle for either your automatic thoughts or those you consciously work up. You can choose precisely what you will think about.

Here are some typical thoughts that will probably enter your mind at one time or another:

"My spouse will never change. He/she will always be that kind of a person."

"I can never meet my spouse's needs."

"If I bring up that subject, my spouse will just get mad again."

"If I share what really happened, I'll never be trusted again."

"Why bother asking him/her to share his/her feeling? He/she will only clam up again."

"He hates me."

"I just know there's an affair going on."
"He's so inconsiderate! Why doesn't he grow up!"
"I must have everything perfect in my house."

What Do You Think?

What thoughts come into your mind? List them below.

1.

2.

3.

4.

5.

6.

When a thought comes into your mind, what do you do with it? A negative or angry thought, when not challenged, intensifies and expands. In 1 Peter 1:13 we are told to "gird your minds for action." "Gird" requires mental exertion. Peter says that we are to eliminate or cast out of our minds any thoughts that would hinder growth in our Christian life. This in turn will affect our married life.

What Do You Think?

What would you do to change the thoughts you listed above?

What do you do to change your own thoughts? Question and challenge them.

On paper answer these three questions:
1. Which of the automatic thoughts listed above are true?
2. How do I know whether they are true or false?
3. What are some alternative ways of thinking?

Remember, in answering your automatic thoughts, there are different interpretations for each situation. Some interpretations are closer to fact than others; therefore, you should develop as many interpretations as possible. Often we confuse our thoughts with facts, even when the two do not necessarily relate. Questioning your negative and automatic thoughts will help you create a new form of thinking.

Here is a list of twenty questions which can be very helpful in learning this new art of challenging our thoughts.

1. *What is the evidence?* Ask yourself the question, "Would this thought hold up in a court of law? Is it circumstantial evidence?" Just because your husband missed calling you when he was late for dinner one day does not mean that you cannot count on him for anything. Just because you tripped walking into your Sunday School class and everyone laughed does not mean that you will trip again or that they think you are a clod.

2. *Am I making a mistake in assuming what causes what?* It is often difficult to determine causes. Many people worry about their weight, and if they gain weight they make the assumption that "I don't have any willpower." But is that the only reason? Could there be other causes such as glandular imbalance, using eating as a means to deal with unhappiness, etc.? We do not know the causes of obesity for certain. The medical profession is still studying the problem.

3. *Am I confusing a thought with a fact?* Do you say, "I've always failed before so why should this be any different?" Calling yourself a failure and then believing your name-calling does not mean that the label you've given yourself is accurate. Check out

the facts with yourself and with others.

4. *Am I close enough to the situation to really know what is happening?* You may have the thought, "My wife's parents do not like me and would probably like her to leave me." How do you know what they are thinking? Is your source of information accurate? How can you determine the facts?

5. *Am I thinking in all-or-none terms?* Many people see life as black or white. The world is either great or lousy. Men are either all good or all bad. All people are to be feared. Again where did you get this idea? What are the facts?

6. *Am I using ultimatum words in my thinking?* "I must always be on time or no one will like me." That is an unfair statement to make about yourself or anyone else.

7. *Am I taking examples out of context?* A woman overheard one instructor talking to another instructor about her. She thought the instructor said she was rigid, pushy, and dominant. Fortunately, she checked out the conversation with one of the instructors and discovered that she had been described as having high standards and determination. The words were spoken in a positive context, but because of her tendency to think the worst, distortion occurred.

8. *Am I being honest with myself?* Am I trying to fool myself or make excuses or put the blame on others?

9. *What is the source of my information?* Are your sources accurate, reliable, trustworthy? And do you hear them correctly? Do you ask the persons to repeat what they say and verify it?

10. *What is the probability of this thought occurring?* Perhaps your situation is so rare an occurrence that there is little chance of your worry coming true. One man had the thought that because he missed work for two days he would be fired. After he challenged the negative thought he said, "Well, I've worked there for several years and have a good record. When was the last time anyone was fired because he missed two days' work? When was the last time anyone was fired?"

11. *Am I assuming every situation is the same?* Just because you didn't get along at the last two jobs doesn't mean that you will not get along at your new one. Just because you messed up a

recipe once doesn't mean you will mess it up the next time.

12. *Am I focusing on irrelevant facts?* Of course your spouse is imperfect and there are problems in the world, and people are physically and mentally sick, and there is crime, etc. What can your sitting around worrying about them or becoming depressed over them do to eliminate these problems? How else could you use your thinking time in a more productive manner?

13. *Am I overlooking my strengths?* People who worry or who are depressed, definitely overlook their positive qualities. They do not treat themselves as a friend. They are hard on themselves and focus upon their supposed defects instead of identifying their strengths and praising God for them. It is important not only to list your strengths but also recall times in your past when you were successful.

14. *What do I want?* This is a question I ask people over and over again in counseling. What goals have you set for your marriage? For your worry? What do you want out of life? How do you want your life to be different? How do you want your communication to improve?

15. *How would I approach this situation if I were not worrying about it?* Would I tend to make it worse than it is? Would I be as immobilized by our communication problems as I am now? Imagine how you would respond if you believed that you had the capabilities of handling it.

16. *What can I do to solve the situation?* Are my thoughts leading to a solution of this problem or making it worse? Have I written down a solution to the problem? When was the last time I tried a different approach to the problem?

17. *Am I asking myself questions that have no answers?* Questions like, "How can I undo the past?" "Why did that have to happen?" "Why can't he/she be more sensitive?" or "Why did this happen to me?" Often questions like these can be answered with the question "Why not?" What if something terrible happens? "So what if it does?" Why spend time asking yourself unanswerable questions?

18. *What are the distortions in my own thinking?* The first step in overcoming errors is to identify them. Do you make assumptions or jump to conclusions? What are they? The best

way to deal with an assumption is to check it out. Look for the facts.

19. *What are the advantages and disadvantages of thinking this way?* What are the advantages of worrying? List them out on a piece of paper. What are the advantages of thinking that people don't like you? What is the benefit of any type of negative thinking?

20. *What difference will this make in a week, a year, or ten years?* Will you remember what happened in the future? Five years from now who will remember that your shirt was buttoned wrong? Who really cares? We believe that our mistakes are more important to other people than they really are. If someone chooses, ten years from now, to remember something you said or did that bothered them, that's their problem, not yours.[2]

To create new interpretations, write down all possible interpretations. List as many as possible—both automatic and conscious thoughts. Challenge each thought and write down new interpretations. Then act on your new interpretations if action is needed.

What Do You Think?

There is yet another way to evaluate and control your automatic or self talk. Take an event that occurred recently in your marriage. Using the chart below, in the column briefly state the "facts and events" that occurred. Then write all of the "inner conversation" statements you made. Write positive, negative, or neutral after each one.

After you complete this, simply describe the emotions and feelings that were activated by your self talk. Then tell what you actually said. Go to the next column when you complete the first.

The next column is a "videotape check." Look at what you wrote under *A* and ask yourself, "If I had made a videotape of this event, would the tape back me up on my description of the facts?" Videotapes record facts—not beliefs or opinions.

Then, *B*, evaluate your self talk. Was your self talk based on fact and objective reality? Under *C*, how would you like to feel the next time a similar situation arises? Remember that these feelings will come from what you *say* to yourself. Then tell what you think you will say based on your new emotional responses.

Then, under #2, write out "What I learned from this experience."

1. Evaluate a recent experience.

A Recent Event	Videotape Check
A. Facts and events	A. Evaluate the facts
B. My inner conversation	B. Evaluate your self talk
C. My emotional consequences	C. How would you like to feel about this?
D. What I said in verbal conversations	D. What will you say next time?

2. What I learned from this experience:

POWER TO CHANGE

What does Scripture say about our inner conversations or self talk?

In the book of Lamentations, Jeremiah is speaking of his depression. His symptoms are very intense and he is miserable. He thinks constantly of his misery which further depresses him. He *chooses* to think this way. "Remember my affliction and my wandering, the wormwood and bitterness. Surely my soul remembers and is bowed down within me" (3:19-20).

He then begins to change his self talk and says, "This I recall to my mind, therefore I have hope" (3:21).

Self talk generates and creates mental pictures in our mind. As mental pictures begin to emerge in our mind our imagination has now been called into action. As we run mental pictures through the panoramic screen of our mind our self talk is expanded and reinforced. Note what others have said about the role of imagination in our life.

> Imagination is to the emotions what illustrations are to a text, what music is to a ballad. It is the ability to form mental pictures, to visualize irritating or fearful situations in concrete form. The imagination reinforces the thoughts, the thoughts intensify the feelings, and the whole business builds up.
>
> The imagination is far stronger than any other power which we possess, and the psychologists tell us that on occasions, when the will and the imagination are in conflict, the imagination always wins. How important therefore that we should vow by the Saviour's help never to throw the wrong kind of pictures on this screen of our minds, for the imagination literally has the power of making the things we picture real and effective.[3]

With practice you can learn to turn your thoughts off and on. To do so you must put things in their proper perspective. The more a person practices control the greater the possibility of immediate control. We do not have to act in accordance with our self talk or our feeling.

The Scriptures have much to say about thinking and the thought life. The words *think, thought,* and *mind* are used over 300 times in the Bible. The book of Proverbs says, "As he thinks within himself, so he is" (Prov. 23:7).

Scriptures indicate that our mind is often the basis for the difficulties and problems that we experience. "Now the mind of the flesh [which is sense and reason without the Holy Spirit] is death—death that comprises all the miseries arising from sin, both here and hereafter. But the mind of the (Holy) Spirit is life and soul-peace . . . . [That is] because the mind of the flesh—with its carnal thoughts and purposes—is hostile to God" (Rom. 8:6-7, *AMP*).

God knows the content of our thoughts. "All the ways of a man are pure in his own eyes, but the Lord weighs the spirits—the thoughts and intents of the heart" (Prov. 16:2, *AMP*). "For the Word that God speaks is alive and full of power—making it active, operative, energizing and effective; it is sharper than any two-edged sword, penetrating to the dividing line the breath of life (soul) and [the immortal] spirit, and of joints and marrow [that is, of the deepest parts of our nature] exposing and sifting and analyzing and judging the very thoughts and purposes of the heart" (Heb. 4:12, *AMP*).

A Christian does not have to be dominated by the thinking of the old mind, the old pattern. He has been set free. God has not given us the spirit of fear, but of power, and of love, and of a sound mind (see 2 Tim. 1:7). Soundness means that the new mind can do what it is supposed to do. It can fulfill its function.

What can you do? Let your mind be filled with the mind of Christ. There are Scriptures that place definite responsibility upon the Christian in this regard. In Philippians 2:5 *(KJV)*, Paul commands, "Let this mind be in you, which was also in Christ Jesus." This could be translated, "Be constantly thinking this in yourselves, or reflect in your own minds the mind of Christ Jesus." The meaning here for the words "this mind be" is "to have understanding, to be wise, to direct one's mind to a thing, to seek or strive for" (see Wuest's Word Studies in *The Greek New Testament* for explanation).

The main thrust here is for the Christian to emulate in his life the virtues of Jesus Christ as presented in the previous three verses. "Complete my joy by being of the same mind . . . . Do nothing from selfishness or conceit, but in humility count others better than yourselves. Let each of you look not only to his own interests, but also to the interests of others" (Phil. 2:2-3, *RSV*).

In verses 6 through 8 another example of Christ is given—that of humility. This humility came about through submission to the will of God. The mind of Christ knew God and submitted to Him. A Christian following Jesus Christ must give his mind in submission to God. Remember in 1 Peter 1:13, we are told to gird up our minds. This takes mental exertion, putting out of our minds anything that would hinder progress. Thoughts of worry, fear, lust, hate, jealousy, and unwillingness are to be eliminated from the mind. This means negative and unrealistic self talk. "Finally, brethren, whatever is true, whatever is honorable, whatever is right, whatever is pure, whatever is lovely, whatever is of good repute, if there is any excellence and if anything worthy of praise, let your mind dwell on these things" (Phil. 4:8).

Remember, your inner conversations will determine your outer conversations!

What Do You Think?

1. How do I treat myself? (Describe.) How will I treat myself this week?

2. Have I ever thought of myself as being a parent to myself? (Describe.)

3. What kind of parent messages do I give myself? (List five.)

4. Do I often treat myself with scorn and disrespect? If so, what are some of my "scornful" and "disrespectful" thoughts?

5. Do I sometimes punish myself? What are my self-punishing thoughts? (List.)

6. Do I expect and demand too much of myself? Again, what am I telling myself along this line?

7. Does the way I treat myself reflect on my concept of God? How would a loving God talk to me about the thoughts I've listed above?

8. Does God treat me in the same manner that I treat myself? If not, how does His treatment differ from mine?

9. What do the following Scriptures say about how I should view myself? (Read them and write your responses to each one.)

Psalm 139:14-16

Ephesians 2:10

Philippians 1:6

1 Peter 2:9

1 Corinthians 4:2-5

2 Corinthians 12:9

Luke 1:37

Psalm 1:1

Philippians 4:6-7

1 John 1:9

Isaiah 40:31

Psalm 32:8

10. What are ten positive thoughts I have about my spouse?

11. What are five positive thoughts I will focus on each day this week concerning my spouse?

12. List several comments I make to my spouse and identify the self talk which generated the thought.[4]

Notes

1. Adapted from Gary Emery, *A New Beginning: How You Can Change Your Thoughts Through Cognitive Therapy* (New York: Simon & Schuster, 1981), p. 54.
2. Ibid. p. 59-63.
3. Alexander White, as quoted by Hannah Hurnard, *Winged Life* (Wheaton, IL: Tyndale House Publishers, 1975).
4. Adapted from Jerry Schmidt, *Do You Hear What You're Thinking?* (Wheaton, IL: Victor Books, 1983), pp. 23-24.

CHAPTER 3

MESSAGES FROM THE PAST

Are you free to communicate the way you want to? Are your thoughts and words a reflection of the way you feel now, or are they locked into a pattern because of past influences?

In America the creed of independence is so strong that we feel a need to achieve our own individual independence. "I am my own person"; "I have risen above my life experiences and my past." It sounds good, but most of us are not nearly as independent and free as we would like to believe we are. Our outer conversations come from our inner conversations. But where do the inner conversations originate?

For many of us, unresolved relationships and issues of the past are still guiding our lives and hampering communication.

Some of us even suffer because of a half-resolved and half-buried past. Because we react and respond to others on the basis of unresolved past relationships, we actually perpetuate those difficulties.

Some of us carry wounds from the past, some carry scars. Some of us have buried our painful memories, hoping those memories never resurrect.

As we grow older our storehouse of memories increases. Our personalities and general make-up are the results of those memories. Many of our feelings of joy, hurt, anger, or delight are tied into how we remember events and experiences.

You and I will remember the same event in a very different way. For example I may remember the enjoyment and delight of a day in the mountains hiking to a lake. You may remember the ten-hour drive, arising at 4:00 A.M. and feeling exhausted for three days. We both experienced the same events but different aspects made an impression.

How we remember an event, and its significance, influences today's responses. Our emotions are closely tied to our memory. Henri J. M. Nouwen said, "Remorse is a fitting memory, guilt is an accusing memory, gratitude is a joyful memory, and all such emotions are deeply influenced by the way we have integrated past events into our way of being in the world. In fact, we perceive our world with our memories."[1]

Much of the suffering in marriages today is caused by memories. The forgotten anniversary, a bitter fight, the discovery of an affair, and numerous other events continue to fester and simmer in our minds. Sometimes we try to hide these memories in the recesses of our minds. A usual response to an undesirable memory is to repress or forget it. Who wants to remember the pains of the past? Let's live as though they did not occur.

Hiding them, however, prevents them from being completely healed. Thus they continue to act as an anchor which we drag along with us as we limp through life. When we bury memories and wounds we bury them alive. And their resurrection comes when we least suspect it. Painful memories must be dredged up and faced for healing to occur.

Buried memories of the past surface anew when we encounter problems in our marriage, and the past may determine how we deal with those problems. Some marry hoping that the marriage will serve as a blotter to eradicate the past. They soon learn, however, that the past sticks with them. Marriage does not change our past—it works in just the opposite way. Marriage can reveal past hurts, and all our efforts to keep those memories hidden may eventually result in a crumbling marriage.

WHERE MEMORIES BEGIN

Where do our memories begin? How might they influence us and our attempts to communicate with our spouses today?

What is the earliest memory you can recall? One of my earliest memories is a series of images which come to mind when I think of a trip I took with my parents across the United States at the age of four.

What are the five earliest memories you can recall?

What is the earliest positive memory you can recall? One which comes to mind was a fishing trip at a creek with my brother and a cousin. We pulled in fish after fish and it was a delightful experience.

What is the earliest painful memory you can recall? A painful memory for me was a spanking I got with a switch because I had misbehaved.

Childhood memories are more than remembrances. Feelings and attitudes from even the earliest of years can determine our present-day responses. Some can enable us to move forward in our life. Others interfere. Bottled-up unpleasant memories conflict with your adult life. Dr. Hugh Missildine describes these memories as the "inner child of the past." This child still seeks to control your life. Part of your discomfort arises because many of the feelings are not unreasonable for a child, but they seem undesirable and unreasonable for an adult.

There are times when we ask "Why do I *say* what I do?" "Why do I *act* the way I do?" "What is wrong with me?" "Why do I feel this way?" We may become angry at ourselves for these feelings. We may even criticize ourselves for these inner feelings. But attempts to deny or repress them only create a greater discomfort. Because we don't share this struggle with others, the difficulty is compounded.

Many of your memories fall into the category of unresolved childhood conflict—your "child of the past." Who usually responds to a child? His or her parents. But what do you do when you're an adult and your parents are not around or are dead? Who parents your "child" then? You do. Whether you realize it or not, you have assumed the attitudes and beliefs of your parents so you respond to yourself and to others the way they did, even though these attitudes are not your own. Thus your communication is not really your own. You respond to life partly as a mature adult and partly as your child of the past.

In becoming your own parent you cling to old patterns from the past because they are familiar. And you give in to them even though they hurt because, to live in the unfamiliar present means breaking free of the familiar. And it takes effort to break away from the past.

Our past emerges more clearly when we marry. Dr. Hugh Missildine has suggested that marriage involves four people and not *two*! There are the two adults who act in the present and the two children who respond because of their family background and memories. This certainly complicates a marriage, to say the least! Without realizing it we carry into marriage hidden aspects of our childhood nature. We all do this even though we have heard the admonition from Scripture again and again: "When I was a child, I talked like a child, I thought like a child, I reasoned like a child; now that I have become a man, I am done with childish ways and have put them aside" (1 Cor. 13:11, *AMP*).

During courtship we try to emphasize our mature adult qualities to impress the other person. But once we are married we relax. We make our new home into a place of comfort and soon feel familiar in our surroundings. Now it becomes an atmosphere wherein we can allow patterns from the past to emerge. Haven't you heard husbands and wives say, "He wasn't like this before we married"? Or "I never saw this side of her before"?

A wife's memory may be of a home that was a showplace. She remembers her mother telling her for years that a good wife keeps an impeccable home. So she never allows her home to be messy. She wants to be a good wife, doesn't she? Her husband, however, sees home as a place of cluttered refuge where neatness and order do not exist! Why? He too has messages and images from the past, and perhaps he is following the example set by his own father. Many of us consciously or unconsciously attempt to duplicate the familiar patterns of our childhood.

The child in us had numerous expectations. How we communicated in our childhood home will be brought into our marriage. In many cases the difference in communication patterns and styles between husband and wife is as complicated as two foreign nations getting together. Dr. Missildine takes this point a step further. "Generally, in order to achieve the 'at home' feeling within our marriage, we treat ourselves in the same way our parents treated us. The old 'at home' emotional atmosphere of childhood is copied as precisely as possible, including any painful attitudes that may have characterized our family life in the past. We frequently even invite our spouse to treat us the way our parents did—unknowingly seeking their approval and depending on their evaluation of us in the same way that we once sought the approval and love of our parents. This is, in a way, what is happening when your spouse refuses, perhaps by default or abdication, to assume responsibility or 'acts like a baby.' "[2]

If we could realize that each of us has both an adult part and a child part within us which is (hopefully) still in a growth stage, we may become a bit more accepting of one another.

What Do You Think?

How can we discover how our past has influenced us? How can we discover our past patterns of response?

1. Evaluate your life by completing your own family history.

a. List what you feel are/were the positive qualities of your father.

b. List what you feel are/were the negative qualities of your father.

c. Describe how you feel/felt about your father.

d. What emotions does/did he express openly to you and how?

e. Describe how you and your father communicate/communicated.

f. Describe the most pleasant and unpleasant experiences with your father.

g. What messages did your father give you about yourself? Were they positive or negative? Please describe.

h. Describe how your father punished or criticized you.

i. In what ways are you different from your father?

j. List what you feel are/were the positive qualities of your mother.

k. List what you feel are/were the negative qualities of your mother.

l. Describe how you feel/felt about your mother.

m .What emotions does/did she express openly and how?

n. Describe how you and your mother communicate/communicated.

o. Describe the most pleasant and unpleasant experiences with your mother.

p. What messages did your mother give you about yourself? Were they positive or negative? Please describe.

q. Describe how your mother punished or criticized you.

r. In what ways are you different from your mother?

2. Describe on the following chart (by drawing a line graph) the history of your personal relationship with your father from

infancy to the present time.

Very Close					
Close					
Distant					
	Birth - 5	5 - 10	10 - 15	15 - 20	20 - present time

What made the relationship close?

What made the relationship distant?

3. Describe on the following chart (by drawing a line graph) the history of your personal relationship with your mother from infancy to the present time.

Very Close					
Close					
Distant					
	Birth - 5	5 - 10	10 - 15	15 - 20	20 - present time

What made the relationship close?

What made the relationship distant?

4. Indicate on the following chart (by drawing a line graph) the history with sibling of the opposite sex closest in age to you.

(If there is none the opposite sex, use the same sex.)

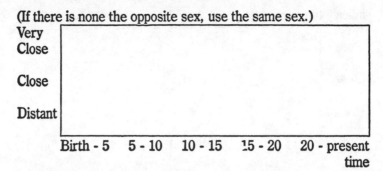

Very
Close

Close

Distant

Birth - 5   5 - 10   10 - 15   15 - 20   20 - present
                                                        time

5. Describe the relationship your parents had as you grew up. Did they openly express feelings? Describe. Did they ever argue or fight? Describe. Was one domineering? Describe. Describe the kinds of difficulties that you sensed between your parents. How did you feel about their relationship?

6. What were you most afraid of as a child (criticism, failure, rejection, competition, darkness, getting injured)? Tell as best you can about the circumstances when you were most likely to have this fear. Give examples.

7. Did you have any Christian training? Describe the role that God has played in your life. What concerns, fears, or problems have you had in relation to God? When were you first aware of them? What have been the most serious concerns for you?

8. List ten adjectives that describe you.

1. _____   6. _____
2. _____   7. _____
3. _____   8. _____
4. _____   9. _____
5. _____   10. _____

Which of these adjectives are characteristic of each of the following?

Spouse _____
Father _____
Mother _____
Brother _____
Sister _____
Friend _____

9. Where on the following line would you place yourself currently in relationship to your parents?

_____

completely   completely
dependent   independent

10. Write out your earliest memory.

One of our tasks as adults is to identify our thoughts and feelings and discover their origin. Recognizing them may be the easiest task; accepting or modifying them will be difficult. Many of these memories (thoughts and feelings) are the bases for how we feel about ourselves. Many of us carry around distorted views of ourselves. These too stem from childhood, continuations of our past which may have been created by longtime parental attitudes. But blaming our parents for who and what we are today has no value. All parents are fallible, we all make mistakes. Most parents do the best they can. We are now responsible for how we continue to treat ourselves.

COMMUNICATION DIFFICULTIES—PAST AND PRESENT

Communication difficulties can be traced to our memories and unresolved childhood patterns. Have you ever wondered why one person is always demanding, asks his/her spouse to perform perfectly, has excessively high standards the other must conform to, and is short on compliments and long on demands and commands? This person may be a perfectionist— you will observe it in his/her behavior and communication. Let's look at this person to see the relationship between the past and the present.

A perfectionist is difficult to live with. If you are this individual, let me illustrate what you probably do. You are demanding of yourself and possibly of your spouse. You exert tremendous energy to accomplish an ever elusive goal. Everything must be in its place; colors must match; every item has to be properly lined up on the table; you must say the right phrase; be punctual; etc. You may give great attention to every little detail and become upset when you cannot regulate all of your life or the life of your partner. The problem is you are never satisfied with your own or with your mate's performance.

You experience success but still feel empty and dissatisfied. You may feel like a "successful failure." Many individuals are successful and proficient, they can rest in what they have accomplished and feel good about their attainment. Often what they do benefits and serves others. They are satisfied. The perfectionist, however, strives for his own benefit and does not find satisfaction. His cry is, "I must do better, better, better!"

A perfectionist probably received parental messages which included: "You can do better"; "That's not good enough"; "Always do better than others"; "You'll receive love if you perform"; "Beat the next guy." We remember comments, words, withheld praise, double messages, sad faces, frowns, signs of disappointment, requests for more this, more that, etc. And thus the treadmill of striving is perpetuated.

The perfectionist has an endless goal of pleasing his parents. They may no longer be around but their parental message is still a recurring childhood memory. This colors the perfectionist's inner conversations and thus how he responds outwardly. Those around him must also perform. "If I must be perfect, so must they. I must urge them on, criticize, correct, make them perfect as I must be perfect. Never let up on them. Everyone can do better." What happens when others slack off and are not perfect? The perfectionist becomes anxious because the lack of perfect behavior in others arouses his own feelings of self-belittlement. His feeling is that no one ever succeeds, including himself. His striving is a desire to escape this constant feeling of "I could have done better."

In relationships, the message is, "You could have done better." There is always the elusive promise of future acceptance if only a better job is done. But it never really occurs. The perfectionist's communication patterns reflect his feelings. By continuing to use the same belittling expressions and statements he undermines himself and his relationships.

We do not need a list of achievements to prove ourselves as persons of worth. When we think of our worth as an achievement rather than a gift we end up on a treadmill. We need not fear losing our worth, because God's estimation of us is not based upon our qualifications. He created us in His image as persons of value and worth. If we feel our worth has to be achieved, then we must be constantly concerned about any threat to our performance.

The perfectionist's fear of failure is a fear of the sense of worthlessness. He has learned to focus more on what he lacks than on what he has. But when we can believe that our worth is a gift from God we are free to risk, for our worth remains stable whether we achieve or not. We are free then to attempt new ventures which could actually enhance this gift of worth. God's act in our life is an emancipation. We are free from the infringement of fearful hesitation and perfectionistic striving.

What Do You Think?

1. In what ways do you need to be declared free?

2. What slave/master messages still bind you?

3. What do you need to ask God to free you from?

Some of us came from yet a different home environment which affects our life and our marriage. Our parents may have thought that the best way to express their love to us was through indulgence. As a child we were given, given, given! Even before we asked, we received. Even if there was no interest or need on our part, material items, attention, and services were provided. A child in this type of home atmosphere has little opportunity to learn satisfaction from his own efforts. The child is almost kept in a dependent passive state and does not learn to take initiative. Instead, he learns to expect others to provide for him and entertain him. You would probably label this person selfish or self-centered.

What kind of messages does this child receive? He believes

that others will and should provide for him. He doesn't have to do much to receive attention, affection, gifts, etc. He demands whatever he wants and feels little need to provide anything in return. He is generally passive with high expectations of others. How will these childhood messages and memories affect marriage? Watch and see.

An overindulged partner expects his/her spouse to be a mind reader, and when the spouse isn't, he/she complains—not always outwardly but in his inner conversations. He feels frustrated, annoyed, restless, and hurt. When the complaints do come they may sound like this:

"My wife ought to know I like . . . "

"My wife should know how I'm feeling . . . "

"My husband ought to do most of the housework for me so I could go out . . . "

"Why should I tell him? If he truly loves me he should know what I want."

This person is a taker but not a giver. Intimacy and emotional involvement in marriage cannot develop. He has no concern over disappointing his partner. He resists any efforts on the part of his partner to become a contributing member of the marriage. He will find many ways of escaping giving.

These are just two brief illustrations of how our childhood is still with us. There are many other ways in which these patterns emerge.

CHANGING THE EFFECT OF OUR MEMORIES

How can the influence of our memories be changed? How can our childhood messages be altered?

Blaming our circumstances or our parents is not the solution. Our parents were human and fallible. We may feel resentment, anger, and bitterness toward them because of what they either did or did not do. But in making them our scapegoat we simply rid ourselves of the responsibility for the way we are today. We *can* do something about the *continuation* of parental attitudes and memories which continue to influence us. For these we *are* responsible. Perhaps if we become a better parent to ourselves we can become a more mature child to our parents.

Nor can we expect our parents to change in order to make our life different. Many of us move through life never having our needs for approval, acceptance, or recognition met by our parents. And we never will. No other person can make up in a few days or even months what we feel we lacked for years and years. To continue to strive to meet parental expectations or to rail against their lack of love is futile. The solution is to come to the place where we can say, "It's alright for this to have occurred. It was painful but I can go on in my life without the influence of the past. It is okay for them to be them and for me to become all that I can."

Joyce Landorf has written one of the most insightful books of our time on this topic, *Irregular People*. An irregular person is a very significant person in our life, possibly a sibling or a parent. This individual is emotionally blind to us and cannot give us what we feel we need from him or her. The irregular person continues to wound us, reinforcing some of the negative messages we've already incorporated into our life. The affirmation we want will not be coming.

In her book, Joyce shares a letter she received from Dr. James Dobson concerning her irregular person. He writes:

> Joyce, I am more convinced every day that a great portion of our adult effort is invested in the quest for that which was unreachable in childhood.
>
> The more painful the early void, the more we are motivated to fill it later in life. Your irregular person never met the needs that he should have satisfied earlier in your life, and I think you are still hoping he will miraculously become what he never has been. Therefore, he constantly disappoints you—hurts you and rejects you.
>
> I think you will be less vulnerable to pain when you accept the fact that he cannot, or will he ever, provide the love and empathy and interest that he should. It is not easy to insulate yourself in this way . . . but it hurts less to expect nothing than to hope in vain.

A GREAT PORTION OF
OUR ADULT EFFORT IS
INVESTED IN THE QUEST
FOR THAT WHICH WAS
UNREACHABLE IN CHILDHOOD.

I would guess that your irregular person's own childhood experiences account for his emotional peculiarities, and can perhaps be viewed as his own unique handicap. If he were blind, you would love him despite his lack of vision. In a sense, he is emotionally "blind." He's blind to your needs. He's unaware of the hurts behind the incidents and the disinterest in your accomplishments, and now Rick's wedding. His handicap makes it impossible for him to perceive your feelings and anticipation. If you can accept him as a man with a permanent handicap— one which was probably caused when *he* was vulnerable—you will shield yourself from the ice pick of his rejection.[3]

Here is part of the answer to freeing us up so that we don't become an irregular person to someone else. Our first step is to accept this person as he/she is, and not to expect the person to change.

The second step is to remember that this person has probably experienced the same negative treatment at some point in life. Now you have the opportunity to break the cycle. The Bible says: "Remember ye not the former things, neither consider the things of old. Behold, I will do a new thing; now it shall spring forth; shall ye not know it? I will even make a way in the wilderness, and rivers in the desert" (Isa. 43:18-19, *KJV*).

Lloyd Ogilvie suggests that "the sure sign that we have an authentic relationship with God is that we believe more in the future than in the past. The past can be neither a source of confidence nor a condemnation. God graciously divided our life into days and years so that we could let go of yesterdays and anticipate our tomorrows. For the past mistakes, He offers forgiveness and an ability to forget. For our tomorrows, He gives us the gift of expectation and excitement."[4]

FORGIVENESS—THE KEY TO A NEW LIFE

"Is it fair to be stuck to a painful past? Is it fair to be walloped again and again by the same old hurt. Vengeance is having a videotape planted in your soul that cannot be turned off. It plays the painful scene over and over again inside your mind. It hooks you into its instant replays. And each time it replays, you feel the clap of pain again. Is it fair?

"Forgiving turns off the videotape of pained memory. Forgiving sets you free. Forgiving is the only way to stop the cycle of unfair pain turning in your memory."[5]

Can you accept your parents for who they are, what they may have done, and for the messages they gave you? This means forgiving to the point that you no longer allow what has occurred in the past to influence you anymore. Only by doing this can you be free—free to develop yourself, to experience life, to communicate in a new way, free to love yourself and your spouse.

Lloyd Ogilvie asks the question: "Who's your burden? Whom do you carry emotionally, in memory, or in conscience? Who causes you difficult reactions of guilt, fear, frustrations, or anger? That person belongs to God. He's carrying him or her too, you know! Isn't it about time to take the load off, face the unresolved dynamics of the relationship, and forgive and forget?"[6]

Not forgiving means inflicting inner torment upon ourselves. When we reinforce those parental messages we make ourselves miserable and ineffective. Forgiveness is saying, "It is all right, it is over, I no longer resent you nor see you as an enemy, I love you even if you cannot love me back."

Then we need to ask for a renovation of our memory. We cannot forget but we can remember factually and not emotionally.

Perhaps Webster's definition of forget would give us some insight into the attitude and response we can choose. Forget means "to lose the remembrance of . . . to treat with inattention or disregard . . . to disregard intentionally: overlook: to cease remembering or noticing . . . to fail to become mindful at the proper time."

Scripture gives us our guiding pattern for this process.
• Don't keep score anymore. "[Love] does not act unbecomingly; it does not seek its own, is not provoked, does not take

into account a wrong suffered" (1 Cor. 13:5).

• Develop a greater love for the Word of God which will allow you *not* to be offended. "Those who love Thy law have great peace, and nothing causes them to stumble" (Ps. 119:165).

• Refuse to hang onto a judgmental attitude. "Do not judge lest you be judged yourselves. For in the way you judge, you will be judged; and by your standard of measure, it shall be measured to you. And why do you look at the speck in your brother's eye, but do not notice the log that is in your own eye? Or how can you say to your brother, 'Let me take the speck out of your eye,' and behold, the log is in your own eye? You hypocrite, first take the log out of your own eye, and then you will see clearly enough to take the speck out of your brother's eye" (Matt. 7:1-5).

As you learn to forgive you will be able to accept your past for what it was and go on.

> Resignation is surrender to fate.
> Acceptance is surrender to God.
> Resignation lies down quietly in an empty universe.
> Acceptance rises up to meet the God who fills that universe with purpose and destiny.
> Resignation says, "I can't."
> Acceptance says, "God can."
> Resignation paralyzes the life process.
> Acceptance releases the process for its greatest creativity.
> Resignation says, "It's all over for me."
> Acceptance asks, "Now that I'm here, what's next, Lord?"
> Resignation says, "What a waste."
> Acceptance asks, "In what redemptive way will you use this mess, Lord?"
> Resignation says, "I am alone."
> Acceptance says, "I belong to you, O God."[7]

RECALLING POSITIVE MEMORIES

Negative memories and parental messages are a part of life. But what are the good memories? They are there but perhaps they have lain dormant. During difficult times and distress, good memories can bring hope and positive response. Can you recall specific times when you experienced trust, love, forgiveness, acceptance, and hope?

Perhaps we, like the children of Israel, need to be called back to positive memories. Moses reminded the people to "remember how the Lord your God led you all the way in the desert . . . Observe the commands of the Lord your God, walking in his ways and revering him" (Deut. 8:2,6, *NIV*). "Do not mistreat strangers, remember that once you were a stranger" (see Exod. 22:21). Isaiah urged the people to "remember the former things long past. For I am God, and there is no other . . . like Me" (Isa. 46:9).

Remembering who we are in the sight of God can, in time, become a stronger memory overshadowing the negative memories from the past. God asks us to remember, to refocus our attention, to challenge our negative way of responding to life and correct it. How is this done?

First, *change the direction of your thought life and remembrances.* "Be anxious for nothing, but in everything by prayer and supplication with thanksgiving let your requests be made known to God. And the peace of God, which surpasses all comprehension, shall guard your hearts and your minds in Christ Jesus. Finally, brethren, whatever is true, whatever is honorable, whatever is right, whatever is pure, whatever is lovely, whatever is of good repute, if there is any excellence and if anything worthy of praise, let your mind dwell on these things" (Phil. 4:6-8).

Second, *identify your parental attitudes and your present reaction to them.*

Third, *identify the belittling comments which you make to yourself and challenge them.*

Fourth, *if you are a perfectionist, as you see yourself striving a little too hard, force yourself to stop sooner.* Lower expectations and reduce your efforts. At the same time keep telling yourself that you have done enough. That you are worth more than your efforts and results. Recall the values and worth you have because of God's view of you. The overindulged person's efforts, on the other hand, need to be increased. Spend more time meeting the needs of others. Become a giver.

Fifth, *commit yourself to treat yourself in a new, positive way, and not as you have treated yourself in the past.*

The more we incorporate the biblical perspective of ourselves into our consciousness, the easier it will become to overcome hurtful memories and crippling messages. For it is God that does it in us.

Who are we? How does God see us? He sees us as being worth the precious blood of Jesus. "Or do you not know that your body is a temple of the Holy Spirit who is in you, whom you have from God, and that you are not your own? For you have been bought with a price: therefore glorify God in your body" (1 Cor. 6:19-20). "Knowing that you were not redeemed with perishable things like silver or gold from your futile way of life inherited from your forefathers, but with precious blood, as of a lamb unblemished and spotless, the blood of Christ" (1 Pet. 1:18-19). "And they sang a new song, saying, 'Worthy art Thou to take the book, and to break its seals; for Thou wast slain, and didst purchase for God with Thy blood men from every tribe and tongue and people and nation" (Rev. 5:9).

God knows us through and through! He is fully aware of us. "And the Lord said to Moses, . . . 'you have found favor in My sight, and I have known you by name' " (Exod. 33:17). "Before I formed you in the womb I knew you, and before you were born I consecrated you" (Jer. 1:5). "I am the good shepherd; and I know My own, and My own know Me, . . . and I lay down My life for the sheep . . . . My sheep hear My voice, and I know them . . . and they shall never perish" (John 10:14-15, 27-28).

Dr. James Packer writes, "There is tremendous relief in knowing that His love to me is utterly realistic, based at every point on prior knowledge of the worst about me, so that no discovery now can disillusion him about me, in the way I am so often disillusioned about myself, and quench His determination to bless me . . . He wants me as His friend, and desires to be my friend, and has given His Son to die for me in order to realize this purpose."[8]

The times in our lives when we are at peace with ourselves,

not bound by the past, are the times when we feel as though we belong. We feel wanted, desired, accepted, enjoyed. We feel worthy: "I count." "I am good." We also feel competent: "I can do it."

These feelings are essential for they work together to give us our sense of identity. But the times of feeling complete may be all too infrequent. Now is the time to remember our roots, our heritage.

We are created in the image of God. He wants His work to be complete in us. When we relate to His Son Jesus Christ by faith, we have the potential for a sense of inner wholeness (see Col. 2:10).

In our relationship to God we can be assured that we belong to Him. Dr. Maurice Wagner suggests that "we never outgrow the need for a parent even though we may be parents ourselves." We are responsible to God, and we relate to Him as our heavenly Parent. There is deep emotional satisfaction in relating to God as Father. For He is a Father as a father should be.

Perhaps the greatest security to be found is in the sense of parental acceptance. We read, "He [the Father] hath made us accepted in the beloved [Christ]" (Eph. 1:6). We did absolutely nothing to earn that acceptance; we submitted to Him, and He made us accepted to Himself! "God so loved the world, that He gave His only begotten Son" (John 3:16). He made us accepted because He loved us!

He is pleased to call us His sons. That gives us a position with Him in His family. We know we are somebody to God; we have been redeemed from being a nobody!

In our relationship with the Son of God we are assured of worthiness. Being forgiven all sin, we lose our sense of guilt and the associated feelings of being a nobody, a bad person.

We also have a secure sense of competence as we relate to the Holy Spirit as our Comforter, Guide, and Source of strength. He is with us daily to face our situations with us, and He is in sovereign control of the situations that He allows us to experience.

He imparts the ability to live a godly life and maintain a relationship with God in spite of the undertow of habit and the emotional insecurities we derived from our childhood. He is our competence, making it possible to live the Christian life and hold onto the sense of being somebody in God.[9]

This is the beginning for new growth—new memories. New messages to ourselves. New self talk. New outward communication and new relationships. It is possible!

What Do You Think?

1. Identify any memories or messages from the past which you want to release. Describe how you will do this.

2. Which passage of Scripture from this chapter will assist you the most with your communication? Describe how this will occur.

3. Describe the memories you wish others to have of you.

4. What do you need to do at this time for them to have these memories?

Notes

1. Henri H. M. Nouwen, *The Living Reminder* (New York: Seabury Press, 1977), p. 19.
2. W. Hugh Missildine, M.D., *Your Inner Child of the Past* (New York: Simon and Schuster, 1963), p. 59.
3. Joyce Landorf, *Irregular People* (Waco, TX: Word Books, 1982), pp. 61-62.
4. Lloyd John Ogilvie, *God's Best for My Life* (Eugene, OR: Harvest House, 1981), p. 1.
5. Lewis B. Smedes, "Forgiveness: The Power to Change the Past" *Christianity Today,* January 7, 1983, p. 26.
6. Ogilvie, *God's Best for My Life,* p. 9.
7. Creath Davis, *Lord, If I Ever Needed You It's Now* (Palm Springs, CA: Ronald H. Haynes, 1981), p. 88.
8. J. I. Packer, *Knowing God* (Downers Grove, IL: Inter-Varsity Press, 1973), p. 37.
9. Maurice E. Wagner, Ph.D., *The Sensation of Being Somebody* (Grand Rapids: Zondervan Publishing House, 1975), pp. 164-167.

CHAPTER 4
COMMUNICATING THE REAL YOU

Now that you realize how your past molds your present thinking, how do you begin to communicate the real you?

Communication is the process of sharing yourself both verbally and nonverbally in such a way that the other person can understand and accept what you are sharing. Of course, it means you also have to attend with your ears and eyes so that the other person can communicate with you.

Communication is accomplished only when the other person receives the message you send, whether verbal or nonverbal. Communication can be effective, positive, and constructive, or it can be ineffective, negative, and destructive. While one spouse may intend the message to be positive, the other spouse may receive it as negative.

The Word of God is the most effective resource for learning to communicate. In it you will find a workable pattern for healthy relationships. Here are just a few of the guidelines it offers:

- "But speaking the truth in love, we are to grow up in all aspects into Him, who is the head, even Christ" (Eph. 4:15).
- "A man who refuses to admit his mistakes can never be successful. But if he confesses and forsakes them, he gets another chance" (Prov. 28:13, *TLB*).
- "For we all stumble in many ways. If any one does not stumble in what he says, he is a perfect man, able to bridle the whole body as well" (Jas. 3:2).
- "Let him who means to love life and see good days refrain his tongue from evil and his lips from speaking guile" (1 Pet. 3:10).
- "Some people like to make cutting remarks, but the words of the wise soothe and heal" (Prov. 12:18, *TLB*).
- "A wise man controls his temper. He knows that anger causes mistakes" (Prov. 14:29, *TLB*).
- "Gentle words cause life and health; griping brings discouragement . . . . Everyone enjoys giving good advice, and how wonderful it is to be able to say the right thing at the right time!" (Prov. 15:4,23, *TLB*).
- "Timely advice is as lovely as golden apples in a silver basket" (Prov. 25:11, *TLB*).
- "A friendly discussion is as stimulating as the sparks that fly when iron strikes iron" (Prov. 27:17, *TLB*).
- "Pride leads to arguments; be humble, take advice and become wise" (Prov. 13:10, *TLB*).
- "Love forgets mistakes; nagging about them parts the best of friends" (Prov. 17:9, *TLB*).
- "Let all bitterness and wrath and anger and clamor and slander be put away from you, along with all malice. And be kind to one another, tenderhearted, forgiving each other, just as God in Christ also has forgiven you" (Eph. 4:31-32).

Communication which is effective depends not so much on what is said but on why and how it is shared. Much of the conversation between married couples is simply conveying information—"I had a rough day at work today"—which is really the least important purpose of marital communication.

Why do we seek to really communicate with one another? For some of us it is a way of achieving empathy with our spouse. We want to know that our partner feels what we are feeling. We want someone to share our positive feelings and our joys, as well as our negative feelings and sorrow. Romans 12:15 exhorts us to do this.

Sometimes, rather than merely conveying information, we desire to draw the other person into our life. When we are encouraged to talk about what happened to us at work, at home, or at church, we feel accepted by our spouse.

Another reason for sharing is to ventilate anger and pain. Not only do we need to express our emotions, we also need someone to listen and accept us. We need a sounding board; however our listener needs inner security and emotional stability in order to be a sounding board.

The foregoing are a few of the reasons why we share with one another, but they all boil down to one basic need—we want to be affirmed and supported by the person we love. This kind of support reinforces our own beliefs or feelings about ourselves. We need positive (not negative) feedback that says, "You are adequate, lovable, good, nice to be around, etc." Marcia Lasswell and Norman Lobenz in their outstanding book *No-Fault Marriage* suggest four levels of support.

Support Level 1 is what we all desire. This is when one spouse is in total agreement with his partner's goals, ideas, or beliefs. Many people feel this is the only type of support that has any value. It is the easiest to give because supporting what one agrees with does not make an overwhelming demand on your love or concern.

Support Level 2 is when you do not agree with what your spouse wants to do, but you will provide support to whatever extent you can. This support is based upon respect for one's partner.

Support Level 3 is sort of a hands-off position. You disagree with your spouse and cannot give any kind of support. But you do not create problems or obstacles for him.

Support Level 4 is really *no* support. Not only do you disagree with your spouse but you attempt to prevent him from doing what he wants to do.

What Do You Think?

1. Give an example of a time when you experienced each support level and tell how you felt.

Support Level 1:

Support Level 2:

Support Level 3:

Support Level 4:

2. In what area of your life would you like Level 1 support from your spouse?

3. How could you express this particular concern to your spouse?

4. In what area of his/her life would your spouse like Level 1 support from you?

WHAT DO YOUR WORDS MEAN?

When a couple marries, two distinct cultures and languages come together. If each of you does not define your words, then assumptions and misunderstandings will occur. A husband tells his wife that he will be home early tonight. What is his definition of "early"? What is his wife's definition? Or when a wife responds to her husband's request, "I'll do it later," what does that loaded word "later" mean? The wife may mean, "I'll do it in three days." Her husband may interpret it as, "She'll do it in three hours."

Nonspecific commitments such as, "I'll think about it," create disagreements and frustration. The response, "Yes, I'll try," is also insufficient. Nothing may happen but the spouse can still say, "But I'm trying." A definite and specific commitment is much more acceptable.

"I will call you if I see that I will be late for dinner."

"I will help clean up the family room starting this Saturday."

"I will help you in disciplining John by . . . "

"I will have dinner ready by the time you arrive home from the office."

"I will begin praying with you, and we will pray together at least three days a week."

A significant question for couples to ask each other is, "To what extent do we both mean the same thing by the words we use?" Two people can speak Spanish and not mean the same thing. Two people can speak German and not mean the same thing. Two people can speak English and not mean the same thing. Our own experience, mind set and intent give meaning to our words. Have you ever experienced one of the following situations?

"Could I talk to you for a minute?" your spouse asks. You say yes assuming your partner means "a minute." Forty minutes later your spouse is still talking and you are becoming agitated and restless.

"Could you please pick up one or two things at the market on the way home for me?" your spouse asks. After you agree you discover that "one or two things" involves four different stops at locations scattered away from your main route home.

You're on your way home with your spouse and he/she asks, "Could you stop at the store just for a minute. I need one item." Thirty minutes later you are still waiting in the car.

Even when we raise our voices when we communicate means something different to each person. Yelling may be a normal form of expression for one person, whereas to the other it means anger and being out of control.

A husband responds to his wife's question of "How did you like the dinner?" with "Fine." To him the word means "Great; very satisfying. I liked it a lot." But to his wife it means he had little interest in what he was eating. If the situation was reversed she would use several sentences and lots of adjectives to describe her delight. He uses a single word. But both people may mean the very same thing.

One of the most vicious and destructive communication techniques is silence. It can be devastating. Each of us needs to be recognized and acknowledged. But when our partner retreats into silence our very presence, existence, and significance are ignored by the most significant person in our lives. In fact, many people would consider such silence an insult!

Silence can communicate a multitude of things: happiness, satisfaction, a sense of contentment, and well-being. But more often than not it communicates dissatisfaction, contempt, anger, pouting, sulking, "who cares," "who gives a darn," "I'll show you," etc. When silence prevails there is little opportunity to resolve issues and move forward in a relationship. "Talk to me," we beg and our spouse gets angry or continues to withdraw through silence. Too many of us use silence as a weapon.

But think about the meaning of silence for a moment. What is silence? It is really a form of communication and if we respond accordingly we may get our spouse to open up. "What do you think about the question I've asked you?" you might say. Or, "Your silence is telling me something. I wonder what you're trying to communicate to me through it?" Or "I'd like to talk to you about your silence and what it does to me. But first I would like to hear what you think about your silence."

Another approach might be, "I've noticed that there are times when it is difficult for you to talk with me. Is there something I am doing that makes it so difficult for you to share with me that you would rather be silent?" If your spouse responds with an answer to this, just let him talk. Do not attempt to defend yourself. Thank him for sharing his feelings with you. If he has not told you what it is that he wants you to do differently, ask him for a suggestion.

WHAT DO YOUR NONVERBALS SAY?

We sing, we cry, we talk, we groan, we make simple or extended sounds of happiness, joy, despair, or anger. This is verbal communication. We touch, gesture, withdraw, frown, slam doors, look at another person. These are forms of nonverbal communication.

Are you aware of the effect your nonverbal communication has upon your spouse? We use gestures, body movements, and eye expressions constantly, but often our awareness of them is minimal. Frequently our words convey a message of approval or permission, but our nonverbals express a conflicting message of disapproval. This means the listener *hears* approval and *sees* disapproval. The result is confusion. Often the listener ignores the spoken message and responds to the nonverbal. Or if he does respond to the words, the speaker becomes irritated and the listener wonders why the speaker is upset.

Body movements provide a basis for making some reasonable assumptions but not for drawing absolute conclusions. It is important, therefore, that couples learn to do the following:

1. Become aware of the nonverbal messages *you* send your spouse.

2. Become skillful in correctly interpreting the nonverbals which your spouse sends you.

3. Develop a fluency in your nonverbal skills.

4. Learn how to bring your nonverbal communication and your spoken communication into harmony.

Nonverbal communication is similar to a code. We need to learn to decipher it, modify, refine, and enhance it. Tone of voice and inflection add another element to the communication process. The mixture can be rather complicated.

What Do You Think?

1. Let's consider what some nonverbal or voice behaviors might mean. Look at the following list and try to give two or three meanings to each behavior.

a. A child nods his head up and down.

b. A person turns her head rapidly in a certain direction.

c. A person smiles slightly.

d. A person's lower lip quivers slightly.

e. A person speaks in a loud, harsh voice.

f. A person speaks in a low, monotonous voice.

g. A person suddenly opens his eyes wide.

h. A person keeps her eyes lowered as she speaks to you.

i. A person speaks in a very halting or hesitant voice.

j. A person yawns during a conversation.

k. A person shrugs his shoulders.

l. A person is sitting rigid and upright in her chair.

m. A person has his arms folded tightly across his chest.

n. A person wrings her hands.

o. A person holds his chair tightly with his hands.

p. A person's breathing is quite irregular.

q. A person starts to turn pale.

r. A person keeps fiddling with his shirt collar.

s. A person slouches in her chair.

t. A person is constantly squirming.

u. A person inhales quickly.

v. A person continuously moves her legs back and forth.

w. A person hits his forehead with his hand.

2. If you would like to know more about the nonverbal behaviors in your family, conduct the following experiment. Make a list of as many of your own nonverbal behaviors as you can think of. Ask each member of the family to do the same project. After you have made your list, indicate in writing what you think each behavior means to the other members of the family. Ask them to do the same. Then discuss your responses together.

3. There are many ways to strengthen your communication skills. Here are some suggestions for both husband and wife:

a. Describe in writing what your spouse does when he/she is telling you by nonverbals that he/she cares for you, loves you, thinks highly of you, etc.

b. Describe in writing your partner's nonverbals when he/she is telling you he/she respects or approves of something you are doing or intend to do.

c. Describe in writing what your spouse does nonverbally when you think he/she does not approve of what you are doing or saying.

d. Describe in writing what you do when you tell your spouse by nonverbals that you care for, love, and think highly of him.

e. Describe in writing your nonverbals when your spouse is telling you he/she respects or approves of something you are doing or intend to do.

f. Describe in writing what you do nonverbally when you think he/she does not approve of what you are doing or saying.

Spend thirty minutes sharing your answers with each other. Give a visual demonstration or example with each statement. This could prove to be very enlightening and entertaining as well.

4. Each of you might keep a written list of the many nonverbals your spouse exhibits over a week's time. At the end of the week sit down and discuss what you saw and what you thought these nonverbals meant. Ask your spouse to clarify uncertain or incorrect meanings.

A wife might share her observations with her husband in the following manner: "Honey, I noticed that there were three mornings this week when the corners of your mouth were turned down and you were rubbing your hands together much of the time. There were also mornings when you were short with the kids and appeared a bit grumpy. When I see these nonverbals it tells me that you are having a grumpy morning. Am I right?"

Or "I've noticed that when you are doubtful about something another person says, you raise and lower your eyebrows and move your head a bit from side to side. Are you aware of this?"

HOW DO YOU ASK QUESTIONS?

The effective use of questions is a tremendous skill for clarifying communication. Avoid questions that begin with "why" because they often create confusion and defensiveness. Questions such as "Why did you do that?" "Why are you so late?" "Why do you always do that?" often produce frustrating answers like *"Because!"* or "I don't know."

A "what" question with its variations—"Who?" "Which?" "When?" "Where?" and "How?"—is far better.

Notice the difference between these two interchanges.

"Why are you unsure of what to say?"

"I don't know. I just am."

"What is it that you are unsure of?"

"I think that I am not certain of . . . "

Using a "what" question does not guarantee a response but there is a greater chance of it happening than if you ask "why?" A "why" question can bring a halt to the communication process. A "what" question is more likely to continue the interchange.

Here is a list of some "what" questions and their uses:

Husband: "I'm not sure I want to go to that church function."
   Wife: *"What* is it that you are not sure about?"

   Wife: "I can't get all these projects done this week, John."
Husband: "All right. What is preventing you from getting them done or at least starting?"

   Wife: "Let's work on that next month instead of now."
Husband: "No. In what way will our situation be different next month?"

Husband: "Boy, I just don't know about that."
   Wife: "What is it that you don't know about? Or if you did know, what do you think your answer would be?"

Husband: "I don't think we will be able to go to your parents this holiday."
   Wife: "Well, what changes or circumstances would it take for us to be able to go?"

   Wife: "I don't believe that at all!"

Husband: "What is it you don't believe?"

Wife: "Let's do that this summer."
Husband: "How will our finances be any different then?"

Go back over all of these examples. Substitute the question "why" for each one. What kind of response would "why" elicit as compared to the response which was given?

ARE YOU VISUAL, FEELING, OR AUDITORY?

Communication means different things to different people. In counseling married couples who are having "communication" problems, it soon becomes apparent that each person has a different communication style. As I mentioned earlier in this chapter, when a couple marries, two different cultures and languages come together. For a relationship to blossom, each must learn the other's language. And each must be willing to use the other's language without demanding that the other person become like him/her.

When people communicate they process their information in different ways. Some people are more *visual,* some are more *auditory,* and some are more *feeling* oriented. Some people think by generating visual images in their minds; some respond from the feeling level; others talk to themselves and hear sounds. (No, they aren't wacky!)

You may be primarily a visual person. You see the sentences that you speak in your mind. Another person responds best to what he hears. The feeling person has a heightened sense of touch and emotion or intuition. He responds on the basis of his feelings.

Each of us has a dominant mode of perception. We have been trained to function primarily in that mode. *But it is possible for a person to learn to function and communicate in the other modes as well.* What are you like? Are you primarily a visual, auditory, or feeling person? What is your spouse? Are you aware of your differences and similarities? Can you communicate or do you usually pass one another in the night?

An easy way to understand the way in which you and your spouse communicate is to pay attention to the words, images and phrases you both use.

What do these phrases say to you?

"I *see* what you are saying."

"That *looks* like a good idea. *Show* me more about it."

"I would like to know your *point of view.*"

"Let's *focus* in on just one subject."

These phrases reflect a visual bias. The person thinks and speaks on the basis of strong visual pictures. Other people see vague pictures, and some no pictures at all.

"I *hear* you."

"Boy, that *sounds* great to me."

"*Tell* me that again."

"That's coming through *loud and clear.*"

"Let's *hear* that again."

These phrases come from a person who is basically auditory. Sounds are of primary importance to him.

"I *sense* that you are upset with me."

"This gun has a good *feel* to me."

"My *instincts* say this is the right thing to do."

These are phrases coming from a person who responds in a feeling mode. Perhaps you have been in a group where a new idea has been shared. If, at that time, you had been aware of these three modes of responding you may have heard, "That idea *feels* good," That idea *looks* good," and, "That *sounds* like a good idea." They all mean the same thing but are presented via three different processes.

What does all this have to do with husband-wife communication? Just this! If you learn to use your spouse's style of speaking *(perceptual mode)* he or she will listen to you. It may be a bit of work and take you a while to become skillful at it but it can work. Too often we expect our spouse to cater to us and do it our way. But if we are willing to take the initiative and move into his/her world first, then we establish a common ground for communication.

There are occasions when you may feel that your spouse is resisting your idea or suggestion. It could be that you have failed to communicate in a way that he/she can understand. If you ask a

IF YOU ASK A QUESTION AND DO NOT RECEIVE THE RIGHT RESPONSE, SWITCH TO ANOTHER WAY OF ASKING THE QUESTION.

question and do not receive the right response, switch to another way of asking the question. "How does this sound to you?" No response. "Does this look all right to you?" No response. "How do you feel about this issue?" A response!

A wife asks her husband to complete a chore. He responds by saying, "Write it down," or "Make me a list." If in the future she makes a list or note and gives it to him at the same time she tells him, she may get a quicker response.

Once you are able to communicate with your spouse in his mode, your spouse may be willing to move into your world. If you learn to see, hear, and feel in the same way that your spouse sees, hears, and feels, communication is bound to improve. We all use all three modes, but one is better developed in each of us than the others.

I have found these principles essential in communicating with my clients in the counseling office. As I listen I try to discover their perceptual mode so that I can enter into their world with them. I listen also to their tone of voice and phrases. I study their nonverbals. Some couples are loud, expressive, gesture a lot, use many nonverbals. Others come in and are somewhat quiet, reserved, very proper, and choose their words carefully. I need to communicate as they do first so that eventually they are willing to listen and move the direction I would like them to move.

Basically I am a visual person, but I have learned to use all three modes. I still prefer the visual, however. If someone brings me a letter or something he has written and says, "Listen to this," my first response is, "Oh, let me see it." I prefer reading it myself rather than listening to it being read. It registers more with me and I digest it more quickly. When I discover some new exciting material that I would like to share with my students, my first inclination is, "How can I diagram this and use it on charts and overhead transparencies so others can see it?" I am more conscious of my tendency to use "visual" words. But not everyone else responds the way I do. Thus I need to broaden my responses to include the auditory and feeling modes. By doing this, others can understand me and I can better understand them as well—and so can you.

What Do You Think?

What can you and your spouse do to develop your communication?

1. Become more sensitive to the words and phrases others use. Listen to a friend or colleague, or listen to someone on TV or radio. Can you identify the person's perceptual mode?

2. Make a list of the various phrases you use during the day. What is your dominant mode?

3. Make a list of the various phrases your spouse uses. What is his or her dominant mode? Practice using that style. You may need to expand your vocabulary so that you are better able to speak your spouse's language. Unfortunately there is no Berlitz language course to teach you this new language. It is something you will have to teach yourself.[1]

Note

1. Adapted from Jerry Richardson and Joel Margulis, *The Magic of Rapport* (San Francisco: Harbor Publishing, 1981).

CHAPTER 5

THE GIFT OF LISTENING

One of the greatest gifts one person can give to another is the gift of listening. It can be an act of love and caring. Too often conversations today between married couples are dialogues of the deaf. If a husband listens to his wife, she feels, "I must be worth hearing." If a wife ignores her husband, he thinks, "I must be dull and boring."

Have you had the experience of being really listened to? Look at these verses from the Word of God that talk about how God listens:

• "The eyes of the Lord are toward the righteous, and His ears are open to their cry. The face of the Lord is against evildoers, to cut off the memory of them from the earth. The righteous cry and the Lord hears, and delivers them out of all their troubles. The Lord is near to the brokenhearted, and saves those who are crushed in spirit" (Ps. 34:15-18).

- "I love the Lord, because He hears my voice and my supplications. Because He has inclined His ear to me, therefore I shall call upon Him as long as I live" (Ps. 116:1-2).
- "Call to Me, and I will answer you, and I will tell you great and mighty things, which you do not know" (Jer. 33:3).

The Word of God also gives us directives concerning how *we* are to listen:

- "He who gives an answer before he hears, it is folly and shame to him" (Prov. 18:13).
- "Any story sounds true until someone tells the other side and sets the record straight" (Prov. 18:17, *TLB*).
- "The wise man learns by listening; the simpleton can learn only by seeing scorners punished" (Prov. 21:11, *TLB*).
- "Let every man be quick to hear (a ready listener)" (Jas. 1:19, *AMP*).

What do we mean by listening? What do we mean by hearing? Is there a difference? Hearing is basically to gain content or information for your own purposes. Listening is caring for and being empathic toward the person who is talking. Hearing means that you are concerned about what is going on inside *you* during the conversation. Listening means you are trying to understand the feelings of *the other person* and are listening for his sake.

Let me give you a threefold definition of listening. Listening means that when your spouse is talking to you:

1. You are not thinking about what you are going to say when he/she stops talking. You are not busy formulating your response. You are concentrating on what is being said and are putting into practice Proverbs 18:13.

2. You are completely accepting what is being said without judging what he/she is saying or how he/she says it. You may fail to hear the message if you are thinking that you don't like your spouse's tone of voice or the words he/she is using. You may react on the spot to the tone and content and miss the meaning. Perhaps he/she hasn't said it in the best way, but why not listen and then come back later when both of you are calm and discuss

the proper wording and tone of voice? Acceptance does not mean you have to agree with the content of what is said. Rather, it means that you understand that what your spouse is saying is something he/she feels.

3. You should be able to repeat what your spouse has said and what you think he/she was feeling while speaking to you. Real listening implies an obvious interest in your spouse's feelings and opinions and an attempt to understand them from his/her perspective.

Failing to listen may actually increase the amount of talking coming your way. Joyce Landorf explains:

> Your wife may be a compulsive talker. Was she always that way, even before you were married? Or did she just seem to get that way with time? Some women talk at the moment of birth and a steady stream follows each moment of their lives forever after, but others have developed a nonstop flow of talk for other reasons. Many times a compulsive talker is really shouting to be heard by someone. The more bored you look, the more you yawn, the more you watch the dog or TV, the harder she talks. She just talks all the more to compensate. You may have stopped listening a long time ago, and she knows that better than anybody.
>
> Do you think this has happened to you? When was the last time that you asked these questions of your wife? "How do you feel about . . . ?" and/or "What happened here at home today?" Do you ever intersperse her remarks with, "You may be right, Hon." If your wife feels you are not willing to listen to her, she has two options: to talk louder and harder; or to talk less and withdraw. Either way, it's very hard on the marriage.[1]

You can learn to listen, for it is a skill to be learned. Your mind and ears can be taught to hear more clearly. Your eyes can be taught to see more clearly. But the reverse is also true. You can learn to *hear* with your *eyes* and *see* with your ears. Jesus said: "Therefore I speak to them in parables; because while seeing they do not see, and while hearing they do not hear, nor do they understand. And in their case the prophecy of Isaiah is being fulfilled, which says, 'You will keep on hearing, but will not understand; and you will keep on seeing, but will not perceive; for the heart of this people has become dull, and with their ears they scarcely hear, and they have closed their eyes lest they should see with their eyes, and hear with their ears, and understand with their heart and turn again, and I should heal them' " (Matt. 13:13-15).

Let your ears hear and see.

Let your eyes see and hear.

The word *hear* in the New Testament does not usually refer to an auditory experience. It usually means "to pay heed." As you listen to your spouse you need "to pay heed" to what he or she is sharing. It means tuning into the right frequency.

Because of my retarded son, Matthew, who does not have a vocabulary, I have learned to listen to him with my eyes. I can read his nonverbal signals which carry a message. Because of Matthew I have learned to listen to what my counselees cannot put into words. I have learned to listen to the message behind the message—the hurt, the ache, the frustration, the loss of hope, the fear of rejection, the feeling of betrayal, the rejection, the joy, the delight, the promise of change. I reflect upon what I see on a client's face, his posture, walk, pace, and tell him what I see. This gives him an opportunity to explain further what he is thinking and feeling. He *knows* I'm tuned in to him.

THREE COMPONENTS OF COMMUNICATION

Every message has three components: (1) the actual content, (2) the tone of voice, and (3) the nonverbal communication. It is possible to express many different messages using the same word, statement, or question simply by changing our tone of voice or body movement. Nonverbal communication includes facial expression, body posture, and actions.

The three components of communication must be complementary in order for a simple message to be transmitted. One researcher has suggested that successful communication consists of 7 percent content, 38 percent tone of voice, 55 percent nonverbal communication.

We often send confusing messages because the three components are contradicting each other. When a man says to his wife with the proper tone of voice, "Dear, I love you," but with his head buried in a newspaper, what is she to believe? When a woman asks, "How was your day?" in a flat tone while passing her husband on the way to the other room, what does he respond to, the verbal or nonverbal message?

A husband, as he leaves for work, comes up to his wife, smiles, gives her a hug and a kiss, and states in a loving voice, "I really love you." After he leaves she feels good. But when she notices the newspaper in the middle of the room, pajamas on the bed, dirty socks on the floor, and the toothpaste tube with the cap off lying in the sink, her good feeling begins to dissipate. She has told her husband how important it is to her that he assume responsibility for cleaning up after himself because it makes extra work for her when he doesn't. But he has been careless again. She believed him when he left for work, but now she wonders, "If he really meant what he said and really loves me, why doesn't he show it by assuming some responsibility? I wonder if he really does love me." His earlier actions contradicted his message of love, even though the message may have been sent properly.

Concerning nonverbal communication, Dr. Mark Lee writes:

> Marital problems may grow out of unsatisfactory nonverbal communications. Vocal variables are important carriers of meaning. We interpret the sound of a voice, both consciously and subconsciously. We usually can tell the emotional meanings of the speaker by voice pitch, rate of speech, loudness, and voice quality. We can tell the sincerity or insincerity, the conviction or lack of conviction, the truth or falsity of most statements we hear. When a voice is raised in volume and pitch, the words will not convey the same meaning as when spoken softly

in a lower register. The high, loud voice, with rapid rate and harsh quality, will likely communicate a degree of emotion that will greatly obscure the verbal message. The nonverbal manner in which a message is delivered is registered most readily by the listener. It may or may not be remembered for recall. However, the communicator tends to recall what he said rather than the manner of his speech.[2]

There are many types of listening. Some people listen for facts, information, and details for their own use. Others listen because they feel sorry for the person. They feel a sense of pity. Some people listen to gossip because they revel in the juicy story of another person's failures or difficulties. There are occasions when people listen out of obligation, necessity, or to be polite. Some who listen are nothing more than voyeurs who have an incessant need to pry and probe into other people's lives.

Some listen because they care. Why do you listen? What are your motives? Any or all of the above? Listening which springs from caring builds closeness, reflects love, and is an act of grace.

Sensitive listening and hearing are open mine shafts to intimacy. Too often the potential for listening lies untapped within us like a load of unmined gold. All of us have barriers which inhibit our listening. Some are simple and others complex.

OBSTACLES TO LISTENING

In order for caring listening to occur we need to be aware of some of the common listening obstacles to communication.

Defensiveness is a common obstacle. We are busy in our minds thinking up a rebuttal, an excuse, or an exception to what our spouse is saying. In doing this we miss the message. There are a variety of defensive responses.

1. *Perhaps we reach a premature conclusion.* "All right, I know just what you're going to say. We've been through this before and it's the same old thing."

2. *Or we may read into his/her words our own expectations, or*

project onto another person what we would say in the same situation. David Augsburger writes, "Prejudging a communication as uninteresting or unimportant lifts the burden of listening off one's shoulders and frees the attention to wander elsewhere. But two persons are being cheated: the other is not being given a fair hearing, and the listener is being deprived of what may be useful information. I want to cancel all advance judgments—prejudgments—and recognize them for what they are, prejudices. I want to hear the other in a fresh, new way with whatever energies I have available."[3]

Two other defensive indicators may be 3. *rehearsing our responses* or 4. *responding to gun-power words.* Rehearsing a response (as well as other defensive postures) is not what the Scripture is calling us to do as a listener. "He who answers a matter before he hears the facts, it is folly and shame to him" (Prov. 18:13, *AMP*).

Gun-power words hook you into a negative defensive response. They create an inner explosion of emotions. Gun-power includes, "That's crude"; "That's just like a *woman* (or man)"; "You're *always* late"; "You *never* ask me what I think"; "You're becoming just like your mother." Not only do we react to gun-power words but we may consciously choose to use some which makes it difficult for our spouse to listen. What are the gun-power words that set you off? What is your spouse's list of gun-power words? Certain selected words can cut and wound.

Not all defensiveness is expressed. Outwardly we could be agreeing but inside we are saying just the opposite. If your spouse confronts you about a behavior or attitude you display that is creating a problem, do you accept the criticism or defend yourself?

Look at the guidance of Scripture:
- "If you refuse criticism you will end in poverty and disgrace; if you accept criticism you are on the road to fame" (Prov. 13:18, *TLB*).
- "Don't refuse to accept criticism; get all the help you can" (Prov. 23:12, *TLB*).

- "It is a badge of honor to accept valid criticism" (Prov. 25:12, *TLB*).
- "A man who refuses to admit his mistakes can never be successful. But if he confesses and forsakes them, he gets another chance" (Prov. 28:13, *TLB*).

Another listening barrier may be attitudes or biases we hold toward certain individuals. These could include people who speak in a certain tone of voice, ethnic groups, the opposite sex, people who remind us of someone from our past, etc. Because of our biases we reject the person or the personality without listening to what the person has to say. In effect we are saying, "If you're ——— (and I don't like people who are ———) I don't need to listen to you."

Our own personal biases will affect how well we listen more than we realize. For example, it may be easier for us to listen to an angry person than a sarcastic person; or some tones or phrases are enjoyable to listen to, whereas others may be annoying; repetitive phrases which another uses (and may be unaware of) can bother us; excessive gestures such as talking with the hands or waving arms can be a distractor.

Some people are distracted in their listening because of the sex of the person who is speaking. Our expectations of what a man shares and doesn't share and what a woman should or should not share will influence us.

We may listen more or less attentively to someone who is in a position over us, under us, or in a prestigious position.

We may assign stereotypes to other people, and this influences our listening to them.

One person hears with optimism and another with pessimism. I hear the bad news and you hear the good news. If your spouse shares a frustration and difficult situation with you, you may not hear him because you don't like complaining; it bothers you. Or you may hear him as a person who trusts you enough to share.

Our own inner struggles may block our listening. We have difficulty listening when our emotional involvement reaches the point where we are unable to separate ourselves from the other person. You may find it easier to listen to the problems of other

GUNPOWER WORDS CAN HOOK YOU INTO
A NEGATIVE, DEFENSIVE RESPONSE.

people rather than your own spouse's. You are hindered by your emotional involvement. Listening may also be difficult if you blame yourself for the other person's difficulties.

Hearing what someone else is saying may bring to the surface feelings about similar problems we are facing. Our listening may be hindered if we are fearful that our own emotions may be activated too much. A man may feel very ill at ease as his emotions begin to surge to the surface. Can you think of a time when in listening to another person you felt so overwhelmed with feelings that you were unable to hear?

If someone has certain expectations for you, you may be hindered in listening to that person. If you dislike the other person you probably will not listen to him very well. When people speak too loudly or softly you may struggle to keep listening.

Do you know what the hindrances are to your listening? Who is responsible for the obstacle? Your partner or you?

You can overcome the obstacles. The initial step is to identify the obstacle. Of those listed, which obstacle do you identify as yours? Who controls this barrier? You or the one speaking? Perhaps you can rearrange the situation or conditions so listening would be easier. You may need to discuss as a couple what each of you can do to become a better listener and what you can do to make it easier for your spouse to listen to you.

Another obstacle which hurts the listening process is similar to defensiveness—it is interrupting. You may erect this barrier because you feel the other person is not getting to the point fast enough. Or you may be thinking ahead and start asking for information which would be forthcoming anyway. Your mind wanders and races ahead. You say, "Hold it. I've got a dozen ideas cooking because of what you said. Let me tell you some of them . . . " It is easy for our minds to wander, for we think at five times the rate we can speak. If a person speaks at 100 words a minute and you listen to 500, do you put your mind on hold or daydream the rest of the time? We process information faster than it can be verbalized, so we can choose to stay in pace with the speaker or let our minds wander.

You may find yourself facing yet another obstacle—overload. Perhaps you have used up all the space available in your mind for information. Someone else comes along with a new piece of information and you feel you just can't handle it. You feel as though you are being bombarded from all sides and you don't have enough time to digest it all. Thus it becomes difficult to listen to anything. Your mind feels like a juggler with too many items to juggle.

Timing is another common obstacle. Have you ever heard comments such as these, "Talk? Now? At 2:30 in the morning?" "Just a minute. There's only thirty-five seconds left in the final quarter of the game." "I'd like to listen but I'm already late for an appointment."

Physical exhaustion presents another obstacle. Both mental and physical fatigue make it difficult to listen. There are times when you need to let your partner know that this is not a good time, but tell him/her when you *will* be able to listen.

Have you heard of selective attention? Another way of expressing this obstacle is *filtered listening,* screening the information being shared. If we have a negative attitude we may ignore, distort, or reject positive messages. Often we hear what we want to hear or what fits in with our mind set. If we engage in selective listening we probably engage in selective retention. That means we remember certain comments and situations and forget those which we reject. David Augsburger describes the process this way:

> Memory is the greatest editor of all, and it discards major pieces of information while treasuring trifles. When I try to work through an unresolved conflict that is only an hour old, I find my memory—which I present as though it were complete, perfect and unretouched—is quite different from my partner's—which I can see is partial, biased and clearly rewritten. We both have selective memories.
>
> Selectivity is an asset. It saves us from being overloaded with stimuli, overwhelmed with information, overtaxed with demands from a humming, buzzing environment.
>
> Selectivity is also a liability. If I deny that it is tak-

ing place there will be much that I don't see, and I won't see that I don't see. If I pretend I saw it all, understood it all, recall it all, there will be many times when I will argue in vain or cause intense pain in relationship with my inability to hear the other whose point of view is equally good, although probably as partial as my own. We each—even at our best—see in part, understand only in part, and recall only a small part.[4]

STEPS TO BETTER LISTENING

How can you become a better listener?

Understand what you feel about your spouse. How you view your spouse affects how you listen to him or her. A partner's communication is colored by how you view him. This view may have been shaped by your observations of his past performance or by your own defensiveness.

Listen with your ears, your eyes, and your body. If your partner asks, "Are you listening to me?" and you say, "Yes" while walking away or fixing dinner or doing the dishes, perhaps you aren't really listening. Concentrate on the person and the message, giving your undivided attention. Turn off the appliance or TV when there is an important matter to talk about; set aside what you are doing and listen.

There are several responses that you could make to indicate to your spouse that you are listening and catching all of what he is saying.

1. *Clarifying* is one of these responses. This response reflects on the true meaning and the intention of what has been said. "I think what you're saying is that you trust me to keep my promise to you, but you are still a bit concerned about my being away just before your birthday."

2. *Observing* is another skill. This response focuses upon the nonverbal or tonal quality of what your partner has said. "I noticed that your voice was dropping when you talked about your job."

3. Another response is called *reflective listening.* A reflective statement attempts to pick up the feelings expressed. Usually a

feeling word is included in the response, such as, "You seem quite sad (joyful, happy, delighted, angry, etc.) about that."

4. *Inquiring* is yet another helpful response. An inquiry draws out more information about the meaning of what was said. A very simple response would be, "I would like you to tell me more if you can."

Be patient, especially if your spouse is a slow or a hesitant talker. You may have a tendency to jump in whenever you can find an opening, finish a statement, or hurry him along. You cannot assume that you really know what is going to be said. You cannot read your partner's mind.

In conclusion, here are Ten Commandments for Better Listening:

   I. *On passing judgment.* Thou shalt neither judge nor evaluate until thou hast truly understood. "Hold it right there, I've heard enough to know where you stand and you're all wet."

  II. *On adding insights.* Thou shalt not attribute ideas or contribute insights to those stated. "If you mean this, it will lead to there, and then you must also mean that."

 III. *On assuming agreement.* Thou shalt not assume that what you heard is what was truly said or what was really meant. "I know what you meant, no matter what you say now. I heard you with my own ears."

  IV. *On drifting attention.* Thou shalt not permit thy thoughts to stray or thy attention to wander. "When you said that, it triggered an interesting idea that I like better than yours."

   V. *On closing the mind.* Thou shalt not close thy mind to opposing thoughts, thy ears to opposite truths, thy eyes to other views. "After you used that sexist language I didn't hear another thing you said."

VI. *On wishful hearing.* Thou shalt not permit thy heart to rule thy mind, nor thy mind thy heart. "I just knew you were going to say that, I had it figured all along."

VII. *On multiple meanings.* Thou shalt not interpret words except as they are interpreted by the speaker. "If I were to stop breathing, would I or would I not expire?"

VIII. *On rehearsing responses.* Thou shalt not use the other's time to prepare responses of your own. "I can't wait until you need a breath! Have I got a comeback for you."

IX. *On fearing challenge.* Thou shalt not fear correction, improvement or change. "I'm talking faster and snowing you because I don't want to hear what you've got to say."

X. *On evading equality.* Thou shalt not over-demand time or fail to claim your own time to hear and be heard. "I want equal time. I want you to feel equally heard."[5]

Listen to your spouse in love. When you listen in love you are able to wait for the person to share his/her thoughts, feelings and what he or she really means.

What Do You Think?

1. List three steps you will take to enhance your listening ability.

2. What topic would you like your spouse to listen to with full attention?

3. Describe an experience in which you feel that God really listened to you. Have you shared this experience with your spouse?

4. Describe how you listen to the Lord.

Notes

1. Joyce Landorf, *Tough and Tender* (Old Tappan, NJ: Fleming H. Revell Co., 1975), pp. 76-77.
2. Gary Collins, ed., *Make More of Your Marriage* (Waco, TX: Word Books, 1976), From an article by Dr. Mark Lee, "Why Marriages Fail—Communication," p. 75.
3. David Augsburger, *Caring Enough to Hear* (Ventura, CA: Regal Books, 1982), p. 46.
4. Ibid., pp. 41-42.
5. Ibid., pp. 55-58.

CHAPTER 6

LIMITING COMMUNICATION POTENTIAL

There are many communication patterns which limit the growth of closeness or intimacy. Sometimes couples simply do not have much to talk about, they have a limited repertoire. This is usually because one person—or both—never learned how to converse. Perhaps he/she never learned to allow others to talk, so he/she tends to dominate conversations. Or perhaps he/she never learned how to express emotions and feelings. Also, some are so limited in education or life experience that their range of topics for discussion is narrow. There are other reasons for poor communication.

BARRIERS TO COMMUNICATION

Sometimes we put up barriers to communication.

Avoiding topics is a common evasive technique. This is when we clearly and openly refuse to talk about a given subject or subjects. We may sidetrack the conversation when the other implies that it is coming up, or we may stop it cold when it does come up:

Wife: What happened at the doctor's office today?
Husband: Nothing.
Wife: You mean to say he told you nothing about your health?
Husband: I don't wish to talk about it. (And, in fact, he does not discuss the topic further.)

Content shifting is when a person changes the subject before any conversation occurs about it. He/she may completely ignore the question:

Wife: What happened at the doctor's office today?
Husband: I've been wondering, how Joe did in school today? Did he get his mathematics test back?

The person who changes topics is attempting to avoid responsibility. He prevents a confrontation by shifting attention to someone else. He may even make counter-accusations. Switching topics is unfair and is destructive to the process of healthy communication. There are three ways to deal with this difficulty.

1. Insist on sticking to the subject at hand but let your spouse know that you are willing to discuss the topic he brought up at a later time. "I'm willing to discuss that later on, but let's continue discussing (the first subject)."

2. Ignore the change in topic and ask for a constructive solution to the situation you are discussing.

3. Respond to your spouse's choice of subject, but come back to the original topic later on. This shows that you are concerned for your spouse's feelings, but it also indicates that the topic which you have raised must be discussed.

Another barrier to communication is *under-responsiveness*— a person says too little in response to a question. A woman who has been having pains in her legs, has a heart condition and arthritis is questioned by her husband. The doctor suspects it's phlebitis.

Husband: What happened at the doctor's office today?

Wife: Not much. He looked at my leg and ankle.

Husband: Is that all?

Wife: He took my blood pressure. (Etc., etc.)

Quibbling occurs when a person tries to clarify or dispute an irrelevant detail. In this example both partners get involved in the quibbling.

Wife: What happened at the doctor's office today?

Husband: I didn't go to the doctor's office today.

Wife: You did too.

Husband: No, I went yesterday.

Wife: I thought it was today.

Husband: No.

Wife: Are you sure?

Husband: Positive.

Quibbling often occurs in disputed versions of some past event. Each of us remembers different events with different meaning.

Wife: You came home at 1:30 that night!

Husband: Oh, no! It was 11:30. I remember you were still watching that program.

Wife: No. I looked at the clock. Besides, you know you don't remember well.

A strange form of communication distraction occurs when a person talks about something whose relationship to the immediate focus of the discussion is not clear. The discussion may involve *irrelevant examples* or ideas.

Wife: What happened at the doctor's office today?

Husband: Yes, I went to the doctor today. He said my blood pressure was a little high. I had a good lunch, turkey and stuffing. Gravy was not too good though. My heart is okay. Says I'm too fat. Need more exercise.

Topic overkill is when a person speaks excessively on a topic. A husband discusses a football game at great length. His wife indicates that she is familiar with the game; she is also finished with the subject!

Husband: That was some pass to Jones in the end zone. He was
   wide open. No one around. What a play!

Wife: Yes, I saw it, you know!

Husband: The pass was overthrown slightly but that guy Jones
   got it anyway. Good hands—and he runs fast. A very cru-
   cial play.

Wife: (Silence.)

Husband: It was fourth down, too, just fifteen seconds left
   before the half . . . (etc., etc.)

   Over-responsiveness involves a person speaking too long on a
subject. What he says goes beyond what is called for in response
to the partner's talk. The partner doesn't have a chance to
respond to specific points, may remember only a portion of what
is said, and may wish he hadn't asked about it in the first place!

Wife: Harry, how do I recognize the Smiths' house when I get to
   Pine Street?

Husband: Well, it's halfway down the first block, on the left side.
   I think the drive is on the right, with a walk made out of
   bricks. Yes, it's painted dark green and has a mailbox in
   front with their name on it.

Wife: Are there other green houses on the street?

Husband: No, just that one.

Wife: Oh, that's all I needed to know.

DEFECTIVE COMMUNICATION PATTERNS

   In addition to barriers to communication described above,
there are such things as defective communication patterns which
can also hinder the development of a marriage.

   Interruptions frustrate a partner and indicate that he/she is
not listening. It is important to wait and listen while the other
person is talking.

Husband: Well, I think that the best solution would be for you
   to—

Wife: No, I can't go along with . . .

   Fault finding can be deadly! As each person blames the
other, both become angry and intimacy is blocked.

Wife: You shouldn't have gotten so angry at me when I was late.

Husband: Well, I wouldn't have if you had been on time.

It doesn't help to argue about whose fault it was. It is a better use of energy to discover a solution which will satisfy both.

Trying to establish "the truth" is often futile for each one has a different view of how something happened. Neither person will change the other's memory and the ensuing argument will probably just anger both of them.

Wife: You did not come home early, it was late!

Husband: I was home on time. It was only . . .

Sidetracking breeds quarrels. It is important to not be defensive and to focus upon one issue at a time.

Husband: I'm tired of seeing dirty dishes on the sink all the time.

Wife: Well, your desk is always messy too, you know.

Then there is the *overload of complaining*. It is better to work on one issue at a time.

Wife: Well, you leave the tub full of water, clothes on the floor, the beds unmade, dishes in the sink, etc.

Placing *guilt* on the other person implies that the spouse is horrible and insensitive. Anger expressed in this guilt-producing manner creates dissension.

Wife: You just don't care about my feelings. You hurt me and you don't even care . . .

Giving ultimatums will push a spouse into a corner. He can either give in and lose face or act strong and tell you to go ahead and carry out your threat. Both breed resentment.

Husband: You do that, and I'll leave, or I'll . . .

Gun-power words such as *always* and *never* elicit a defensive response. The person being accused will remember *one* occasion when he did respond in the proper manner. A useless time-consuming argument will probably be the end result.

Wife: You never come home when you say you will.

Name-calling or *labeling* implies that the person cannot change. It is a surefire way to create anger.

Husband: You're just insensitive and undersexed.

A better way is to share with your spouse the specific behavior that you would like to see changed.

Justifying isn't always necessary. You don't have to justify or give reasons for your likes and dislikes. If you don't like something, just say you don't. Giving reasons often perpetuates a problem because now the person can attack your reasons as well as your actions. In giving your reasons you hand over control to your spouse.

Wife: I don't want to go to the mountains for our vacation. As we've discussed before, I don't like heights.

Husband: Why not?

Wife: I don't know, I just . . .

Mind reading occurs when you tell your spouse you know what he or she is thinking. We feel resentful when someone presumes to be an authority on what we are like internally.

Wife: You think I spend too much money.

Confusing messages: creates mistrust in any relationship. When you verbally agree but your body language conveys the opposite, what is a person to believe?

Wife: Okay, if that's what you want (sigas and rolls eyes).

What Do You Think?

1. Which of these communication difficulties occur frequently in your own relationship?

2. What will you do specifically to change any of these patterns?

3. What Scriptures would help you develop a new pattern of communication?

CRITICAL COMMUNICATION TIMES

There are two extremely critical times for communication between a husband and wife. Both times involve only four minutes! That's all. They are the first four minutes upon awakening in the morning and the first four minutes when you're reunited at the end of the day. These eight minutes can set the tone for the day and the evening. This is a time when couples can share their love and concern, their interests, and can affirm one another, or, they can be angry, curt, critical, or indifferent and adversely

affect the rest of the day or evening.

Examine the patterns which you have established in your marriage. Do you say the same things to each other morning after morning and evening after evening? Think about the way you have responded to each other each morning for the past week and compare your responses with this list.

The Silent Partner—"Don't expect me to talk until I've had my third cup of coffee," he groans as he rejects his wife's attempts at friendliness. He is unaware of his grumpy attitude and places his faith in a magic chemical guaranteed to soothe his disposition.

The Commander—He awakens giving orders. His spouse feels as though she should salute. "Okay, we have ten minutes to get into the kitchen. I want scrambled eggs, crisp bacon, and half a grapefruit. Come on, get up. You take a shower first. I'll give you eight minutes. Then I'll shave, etc., etc."

Compulsive Groomer—She leaps out of bed as the alarm rings, and rushes to the bathroom. Her spouse is not allowed to see her or touch her until she has combed her hair, brushed her teeth and rinsed her mouth. It's probably a syndrome that originated in a TV commercial.

Efficiency Expert (her)—"You know, George, I tell you every morning, if you'd wake up at seven instead of seven-thirty, you'd have five minutes for your hot shave, seven minutes to shower, six minutes to shine your shoes, eight minutes to dress and four minutes to comb your hair. Then you could come to the kitchen just as I'm putting the eggs on the table. Now, why don't you listen? I tell you this every morning."

Efficiency Expert (him)—"You know, Helen, if you get up twelve minutes earlier, you could have the coffee ready by the time I was through shaving. Then while I showered and dressed, you could make my lunch and finish making breakfast. We could chat for three minutes and I'd be in the car by seven-fifteen."

Affectionate Aficionado—"Come on, honey, don't pull away; you know I enjoy making love in the morning. The kids can wait a few minutes for breakfast." Not a bad way to start the day if both partners have the same urge and make time for sex without disrupting other routines. Obviously, if a couple awaken and embrace, four minutes of kissing and fondling is very likely to launch the day positively.

Trivia Trapper—"Good morning, I'll be home at five today. Have dinner ready because I have a meeting at seven. I left some clothes for the cleaners on the chair by the window. Don't forget to renew our subscription to *Time,* and have the mail sorted by the time I get home, please . . . " A guaranteed way to make your spouse feel like a hired hand.

Panic-Stricken Pessimist—"Oh, this is Wednesday. What a terrible day it's going to be. I have a deadline to meet (or three kids to drive three different places) and I haven't even started. I hate Wednesdays!" Tuesdays, Mondays, or even Sundays can also be equally cursed.

The Complainer—"Jean, did you know I've been up all night? These sheets are filthy; why weren't they changed? And there's dust all over the nightstand. When are you going to learn how to clean?" On the other hand, Jean might open the day with: "Jim, did you know I didn't sleep a wink? It's all those rotten bills we haven't paid. Why can't we balance our budget? Haven't you asked for a raise yet? I'm going crazy thinking about money, and I need a new dress for the Carsons' party."[1]

Discuss together your morning routine. Is this a time when you want closeness and intimacy, or would you prefer quiet and privacy? Try making your routine something that is satisfying to both of you and which brings you feelings of love and affirmation.

The second important time of the day has a significant impact on a couple's relationship. What happens during the first four minutes when you and your spouse are reunited at the end of the day? Is it a time of factual reports about the news, the weather, the kids' misbehavior, or other bad news? Is it a time of silence?

Some spouses complain that the family dog gets more attention than they do! And it may be true. Dogs are talked to, caressed, patted; they get their ears rubbed and their back and chin scratched. Not a bad way to greet your spouse! Touching, asking feeling questions, expressing happiness in seeing the other person should make the evening better.

A positive greeting between husband and wife can have a positive impact on other family members as well. Here are several steps to take to enhance your evening.

1. When you see each other at the end of the day give each other your undivided attention and listen with your eyes as well as your ears.

2. Don't come in with a task-oriented checklist of "Did you do . . . ?" Your spouse may end up feeling like the hired hand.

3. Touch, kiss, hug, hold—whatever is pleasing to both of you.

4. Don't make your first statement to your spouse a complaint. It will put a damper on his anticipation of seeing you.

5. Create a relaxing time. Don't immediately hit your spouse with a list of chores to do. Don't breeze in and head directly for the phone, workbench or hobby.

6. Prepare yourself mentally to greet your spouse. Spend time thinking of what you will say and do. Rehearse it in your mind. At least one night a week plan a surprise greeting—something you rarely do or have never done before.

7. Attempt to look appealing to your spouse. A quick combing of the hair or swish of mouthwash will be appreciated.

8. You could phone one another before you leave work for the day. During this time you could discuss who has the greatest need to be met when you arrive home. Some days a wife may need a half-hour relief from the kids to restore her sanity. Both of you may need a half-hour to clear your mind (after the initial four minutes) before you're human again. You might even discuss how you would like to be greeted as you reunite at the end of the day.

COMMUNICATION RULES AND GUIDELINES

All of us have rules we abide by in communication and in resolving conflict. But seldom do we define or verbalize them. Some rules are positive and healthy. Others are negative, detrimental, and continue to perpetuate communication problems.

If married couples would take the time to develop specific guidelines for communication and agree to follow them, communication could become a very positive experience. These guidelines help especially when there are differences of opinion.

A few years ago as I was working with a couple in premarital counseling, I discovered that they were having a bit of a struggle in the area of conflict. I suggested they develop a communication covenant to follow in their conversations. The next week they returned with several guidelines. I sent them out with the assignment to detail the steps involved in implementing each guideline. They returned with their list and then we spent some time refining and revising it.

Here is their unedited covenant. Would these guidelines work for you in your marriage?

COMMUNICATION COVENANT

This covenant will be read together each Sunday and then we will ask one another in what way can we improve our application of this covenant in our daily life.

1. We will express irritations and annoyances we have with one another in a loving, specific, and positive way rather than holding them in or being negative in general.
   A. I will acknowledge that I have a problem rather than stating that you are doing such and such.
   B. I will not procrastinate by waiting for the right time to express irritations or annoyances.
   C. I will pinpoint to myself the reason for my annoyances. I will ask myself why is it that I feel irritation or annoyance over this problem.
2. We will not exaggerate or attack the other person during the course of a disagreement.
   A. I will stick with the specific issue.
   B. I will take several seconds to formulate my words so that I can be accurate.
   C. I will consider the consequences of what I say before I say it.
   D. I will not use the words always, all the time, everyone, nothing, etc.
3. We will attempt to control the emotional level and intensity of arguments. (No yelling, uncontrollable anger, hurtful remarks.)
   A. We will take time-outs for calming down if either of us feel that our own anger is starting to elevate too much. The

minimum amount of time for a time-out will be one minute and the maximum ten minutes. The person who feels he needs a greater amount of time in order to calm down will be the one to set the time limit. During the time-out each person, by themselves and in writing, will first of all define the problem that is being discussed. Secondly, the areas of agreement in the problem will be listed and then the areas of disagreement will be listed, and then three alternate solutions to this problem will be listed. When we come back together the person who has been most upset will express to the other individual "I am interested in what you have written during our time-out and I am willing and desirous of you sharing this with me."

B. Before I say anything I will decide if I would want this same statement said to me with the same words and tone of voice.

4. We will "never let the sun go down on our anger" or never run away from each other during an argument.

A. I will remind myself that controlling my emotional level will get things resolved quicker and make one less inclined to back off from the problem.

B. I am willing to make a personal sacrifice.

C. I will not take advantage of the other by drawing out the discussion. If we have discussed an issue for 15 minutes then at that time we will then take a time-out and put into practice the written procedure discussed under #3.

5. We will both try hard not to interrupt the other person when he/she is talking. (As a result of this commitment, there will be no need to keep reminding the other person of their responsibility, especially during an argument.)

A. I will consider information that will be lost by interrupting the other person.

B. It is important that the person talking should be concise and to the point.

C. I will remember that the person that was interrupted won't be able to listen as well as if I had waited for my turn.

D. I will put into practice Proverbs 18:13 and James 1:19.

6. We will carefully listen to the other person when he/she is talking (rather than spending that time thinking up a defense).
   A. If I find myself formulating my response while the other person is talking I will say, "Please stop and repeat what you said because I was not listening and I want to hear what you were sharing."
   B. If we are having difficulty hearing one another then when a statement is made we will repeat back to the other person what we heard them saying and what we thought they were feeling.
7. We will not toss in past failures of the other person in the course of an argument.
   A. I will remind myself that a past failure has been discussed and forgiven. True forgiveness means it will not be brought up to the other person again.
   B. I will remind myself that bringing up a past failure cripples the other person from growing and developing.
   C. If I catch myself bringing up a past failure I will ask the other persons forgiveness and I will then state what it is that I am desirous that the other person will do in the future and I will commit myself to this behavior.
8. When something is important enough for one person to discuss, it is that important for the other person.
   A. If I have difficulty wanting to discuss what the other person desires to discuss I will say to them, "I know this topic is important to you and I do want to hear this even though it is a bit difficult for me."
   B. In implementing this agreement and all the principles of communication in this covenant we will eliminate outside interferences to our communication such as the radio on, television, reading books on our lap, etc. We will look at one another and hold hands during our discussion times.

DATE
SIGNED (HUSBAND)
SIGNED (WIFE)

As I have shared these guidelines with others, some people

have said, "Well, they worked that out when they were engaged. Just wait until the realities of marriage sink in."

Thirteen months after their marriage I saw the couple for their last session as I do with all couples. Halfway through I asked them if they remembered the covenant they had developed previously. They said, "Oh yes, we take it out quite often for review. In fact we went through it two weeks ago and rated ourselves and each other on a scale of 1-5 for each item to see how we were doing. Then at the bottom of the covenant we wrote 'This is what I will do this next week to enhance the application of this covenant.' "

I had no further questions.

What Do You Think?

1. Select three items from this covenant which would help you in your communication.

2. List three of your own guidelines you would like to implement.

3. What passages from Scripture would you like to apply to your communication process?

Many couples communicate as though life is a contest. They challenge each other, compete, and continually resist each other. In our society we are taught to be competitive. We believe there are winners and losers, and it is best to be a winner (at all costs). There are many winners, however, who have won the battles but lost the war. The best way to handle another person's point of view is not to fight it but to try and find some point of agreement with it. This allows you to move along *with* the person instead of confronting him head on. The attitude needed is,

"How can we both achieve some of what we want?" Life is *not* a contest! But often husbands and wives make it that way!

How can you prevent a discussion from deteriorating into a knock-down-drag-out, either verbally or physically? Consider a situation in which a husband and wife are talking about changing their vacation plans. They have been vacationing at the same spot for seven years and the husband is very comfortable with the choice. His wife would like some variety and a more active time. During the past seven years they spent their vacation time eating, fishing, doing a bit of sightseeing and a lot of loafing. Joan has broached her new suggestion to Rick.

Joan: "Well, Rick, what do you think of this suggestion?"

Rick: "Boy, it's new to me. I don't know. It comes as sort of a shock. I've been satisfied with where we've been going and I thought you were. I need to think about this."

Joan: "That's good, Rick, because we should think about it. I know you've been satisfied and so have I. Perhaps we could talk about what it is that we've enjoyed so much and what new possibilities may be available in a new vacation spot. Perhaps we'll find some overlap."

Joan accepted Rick's resistance, but she brought the attention back to her suggestion. Now they can begin to evaluate.

A second step is to agree with any feelings your spouse has expressed. Rick stated that he was a bit shocked. Joan could say, "I can appreciate your feeling shocked (or angry, fearful, confused, rejected, etc.). I can understand that you'd feel that way. I'd probably have similar feelings." Whether you feel that way or not you can validate the other person's feelings. You are not agreeing with facts or ideas. And you can share if you do have similar feelings.

Joan could also express curiosity or interest in what Rick has said. "I'm interested in what you have enjoyed so much about our vacations." Or, "Tell me some more about your feelings of shock. I'm interested in how you think and feel."

Suppose Rick and Joan continue to discuss and Rick begins to share more of his objections.

Rick: "Well, I've really enjoyed the low-key aspect of where we go. It's not busy and it doesn't take three days of driving to get there. We've met some people there who come back each year and I really enjoy seeing them."

Joan: "If I understand you, this place has become a place of relaxation for you, sort of a hideaway with selected people you enjoy."

Rick: "Yeah, I guess that's it. I'm not sure what a change would be like. This is comfortable and I'm not sure a new place would be as relaxing."

At this point Joan could ask Rick what other information it would take for him to consider a change. Very often we tell our spouses only what we want them to know in order to convince them of our new idea.

There is one other principle to follow: acknowledgement and persistence.

Rick: "Why don't we talk about this another time? Or perhaps when we do we could think about it for the following year and follow through with our plans for the same place this July."

Joan: "I can understand that you'd prefer to go to the same place, but I'd like to discuss the possibility of a new location for *this* year."

Rick: "I don't know. Let's table the discussion for now."

Joan: "I can agree to that but let's set a time to discuss it again for this year."

Rick: "Why don't we just wait and see for awhile . . . "

Joan: "I can understand that you'd rather not set a time, but I'd rather we set a time now to talk about this year's vacation."

In this last conversation Joan is acknowledging Rick's reluctance but presses ahead in spite of it. By being carefully persistent, eventually the other person may agree to setting a time to discuss this year's vacation. This approach can work very well when one person tends to wait to delay discussions and decisions.

In conclusion, here are a number of communication guidelines. Read through them and then complete the "What Do You Think?" portion at the end of the chapter.

1. Greet your spouse after a period of being separated

(even if only for a few hours) with a smile, pleasant talk such as a happy greeting, touching and kissing, a compliment, humor, or recounting one of the day's interesting or "success" experiences.

2. Set aside a period of transition between work—or any potentially stressful activity—and other parts of the day. This transition time is designed to provide a "decompression period" so that any pressures, frustrations, fatigue, anger, or anxiety that may have been generated will be less likely to affect marital communication. Some men pray as they drive home, committing the day's activities to the Lord. Others visualize how they are going to respond to each family member. Some couples take twenty minutes when they arrive home to sit in a dimly lighted room and listen to a favorite record with very little talking.

3. Never discuss serious subjects or important matters that involve potential disagreement when you or your spouse are overly tired, emotionally upset, sick, injured, or in pain.

4. Set aside a special agreed-upon time every day to take up issues involving decision making, family business, disagreements, and problems. This "Decision Time" should allow for the relaxed and uninterrupted discussion of all decision-making and problem-solving activities. No other activities should be involved, such as eating, driving, or watching television. Take the phone off the hook. It may also help to set a time limit.

5. Some couples have found it helpful to save all complaints about their marriage, disagreements, and joint decisions for the scheduled Decision Time when these matters are taken up. Jot down items as they arise. When you pose a problem or lodge a complaint, be specific as to what you want from the other person. Do you want anger, defensiveness, resistance, and continuation of the problem? Or openness, cooperation, and a change on the part of the other person? The way you approach the problem will determine your spouse's response.

Example: "You are not involved enough with the children."

Better to say: "I appreciate the time you spend with the children and so do they. I know you have a lot going on but we would all appreciate your evaluating your schedule so you could spend more time with them."

Example: "You are never affectionate."

Better to say: "I enjoy the times when you touch me. I would appreciate it if you would touch me and hold me several times a day and also let me know if you like something I'm doing."

Recognition and praise of what another person has done is necessary to his sense of self-worth. It also opens the door for a person to accept a constructive suggestion.

6. In the decision sessions, try to reach a specific solution.

7. Set aside a scheduled time for noncontroversial marital conversation, every day if possible. Among the topics that could be discussed are: the experiences you each have had during the day or at other times; noncontroversial plans or decisions that involve individual partners; the couple or the family.

8. Each person should have a special "topic turning signal" to signal his or her spouse to change the conversation from a controversial topic. The signal should be an agreed-upon neutral word or phrase.

9. Do not blame your partner. Save matters of complaint and proposed change for the Decision Time.

10. Stay on the topic being discussed until each of you has had a say.

11. Avoid talk about what happened in the past or what might happen in the future if it is potentially controversial.

12. Be specific in what you talk about. Define your terms and avoid overstatement and generalities.

13. Acknowledge the main points of what your partner says with such words as "I see," "I understand," "Yes," "Um-hm."

14. Try to keep the nonverbal aspects of your communication consistent with the verbal message. Don't express compliments with scowls, or an indifferent tone of voice and a pleasing facial expression.

15. Be as accurate as you can in describing objects or events for your partner. Remember you are describing it from your perspective.

16. Praise your spouse for the things he/she says that you like. Use words that you think will be appreciated.

17. Discuss topics with your partner that you know he/she

will like to talk about. If your partner fails to discuss topics to your liking, do not hesitate to suggest that you would like to discuss the desired subjects further.

18. Never exaggerate in order to make a point. If you really want to persuade your spouse, write the subject down and save it for the next Decision Time.

19. Don't mind read or make presumptive statements about what your partner has said.

20. Don't quibble about minor or trivial details.

21. Respond fully but not excessively when your turn comes.

22. Repeat what you think your partner said if you have trouble understanding him or if you think you did not hear what he/she intended.

23. Help each other to follow the rules. Praise your spouse for rule-consistent talking.

What Do You Think?

1. Go back through the list and put your initials by each guideline that you would like to apply in your marriage. After your spouse has done the same, share your selections. Discuss the steps you will take to implement these principles in your marriage. Set a date to evaluate how these guidelines are working.

Note
1. Leonard Zunin, M.D., *Contact: The First Four Minutes* (New York: Random House, 1972), pp. 136-137.

CHAPTER 7

HOW ARE MEN AND WOMEN DIFFERENT?

"Oh, he thinks just like a man!" Betty says in exasperation. "He never seems to really understand what I'm talking about."

Her husband John says, "Look, I try to talk logic to her but she's on another wavelength. Why can't she be logical? In fact, I find most women are like that! They beat around the bush!"

Have you ever heard comments like these? Perhaps you have made similar statements because you have difficulty understanding how your partner communicates. I have heard some people say that they feel like they have married someone from a foreign country. Their spouse's language is completely foreign to them.

How different are men and women in their style of thinking?

In the way they communicate? Or are there any differences? What do you think?

Look below at the list of differences between men and women that has been compiled from various sources. Think about each statement. Do you agree with them?

MALE/FEMALE DIFFERENCES

1. Men and women are very different by nature in the way they think, act, respond, etc. These differences can be complementary, but very often lead to conflict in marriage.

2. A woman is an emotional-feeler; a man is a logical-thinker.

3. For a woman language spoken is an expression of what she *feels*; for a man language spoken is an expression of what he's *thinking*.

4. Language that is heard by a woman is an emotional experience; language that is heard by a man is the receiving of information.

5. Women tend to take everything personally; men tend to take everything impersonally.

6. Women are interested in the details, the nitty-gritty; men are interested in the principle, the abstract, the philosophy.

7. In material things, women tend to look at goals only; men want to know the details of how to get there.

8. In spiritual or intangible things, the opposite is true. Men look at the goals; women want to know how to get there.

9. Men are like filing cabinets. They take problems, put them in the file and close the drawer. Women are like computers; their minds keep going and going and going until the problem is solved!

10. A woman's home is an extension of her personality; a man's job is the extension of his personality.

11. Women have a great need for security and roots; men can be nomadic.

12. Women tend to be guilt-prone; men tend to be resentful.

13. Men are stable and level off; women are always changing.

14. Women tend to become involved more easily and more quickly; men tend to stand back and evaluate.

15. Men have to be told again and again; women never forget!

16. Men tend to remember the gist; women tend to remember details and distort the gist.

What Do You Think?

1. Go back through the list and indicate whether you agree or disagree with each statement. If you disagree, change the statement to read in such a way that you could agree with it.

2. Share your response with your spouse and discuss how you see each other.

3. If a person believes these statements, how would it affect the way he responds to members of the opposite sex?

4. If there are distinct differences between men and women, are these differences because that is the way men and women are created, or are these differences learned and developed?

ACTUAL DIFFERENCES

Are the differences listed really true? And if they are, is that bad or good? Some people have very definite beliefs about men and women. And those beliefs color the way they behave and respond to others, including their spouse. Let's take a look at some of the actual proven differences between men and women. Genesis 1:27 says: "Male and female He created them." Right from the beginning, the Bible says, there was a difference. God wanted male and female to be different. So, first of all, there are numerous physical differences between men and women.

Dr. David McClelland of Harvard concludes that literally thousands of studies show that significant sex differences exist. In all human societies men are larger and stronger than women. The average man is 6 percent taller than the average woman. Also is 6 percent taller than the average woman. Also men average about 20 percent more weight than women. This is caused by greater body bulk, mainly from larger muscles and bones. Large muscles in males permit them to lift more weight, throw a ball farther or run faster than most women. Even at birth the male has more strength to lift his head higher and for longer periods of time than do females. At puberty the difference in male strength is accentuated, largely due to testosterone.

Men have a higher metabolic rate. They produce more physical energy than women and thus need more food to keep the body performing to its full potential. Women are usually a few degrees cooler than men, and may therefore require less food to maintain a constant weight. Men's blood is richer than women's with an average of 300,000 more red corpuscles per cubic millimeter.[1]

Does this mean that men are physically superior to women? Some people draw that conclusion (especially men!). But recent research indicates that women actually possess certain biological advantages when they are compared with men.

- 130-150 males are conceived for every female, but by the time of birth there are only 106 boys to every 100 girls.
- 25 percent more boy babies are born prematurely than girl babies.
- During the first year the mortality rate among boys is almost one-third higher than among girls.
- Circulatory and respiratory infection and digestive diseases affect boys in greater numbers than girls.
- Boys have more genetic defects than girls.

But what about psychological differences? This is the area that affects communication between men and women. People tend to take extreme views on this particular issue. Some say men and women are totally different mentally, and others say there are no psychological or mental differences between the sexes. There are some differences between the sexes but they may not be as extensive as some would like to think. In some areas men and women are very much alike and in some areas they are different.

What Do You Think?

1. Before you proceed in your reading make a list of the ways you and your spouse are different because of sex. Make a specific list of your unique qualities and your spouse's unique qualities.

2. Indicate which of these you think you could change and how you would make these changes.

Stanford University researchers Dr. Carol N. Jacklin and Dr. Eleanor E. Maccoby released a study in 1974 *(The Psychology of Sex Differences)* in which they reviewed and summarized over 2,000 books and articles on the subject. Several conclusions regarding male/female differences were presented:

> Males have superior verbal ability, males excel at visual-spatial tasks, and males are better at math. In addition, the researchers believed that the evidence was sufficient to reject eight myths about sex differences. They concluded that the sexes do not differ in (1) sociability, (2) self-esteem, (3) motivation to achieve, (4) facility at rote learning, (5) analytic mindedness, (6) susceptibility to environmental influences, or (7) response to auditory/visual stimuli. These characteristics are not biological in nature.[2]

Some other differences have been noted as well. Women are more likely than men to express their emotions and display empathy and compassion in response to the emotions of others. Men as a whole are more skillful than women at visually perceiving spatial or geometric features of objects. Females tend to be more anxious than males about risking failure. When they fail they are more likely to blame themselves. When males fail, they tend to blame others.

Culture plays a large part in our determination of what is

masculine and what is feminine. Too many men live by these Ten Commandments of Masculinity (by Warren Farrell).

1. Thou shalt not cry or expose other feelings or emotion, fear, weakness, sympathy, empathy or involvement before thy neighbor.
2. Thou shalt not be vulnerable, but honor and respect the "logical," "practical," or "intellectual"—as thou defines them.
3. Thou shalt not listen, except to find fault.
4. Thou shalt condescend to women in the smallest and biggest of ways.
5. Thou shalt control thy wife's body, and all its relations.
6. Thou shalt have no other egos before thee.
7. Thou shalt have no other breadwinners before thee.
8. Thou shalt not be responsible for housework—before anybody.
9. Thou shalt honor and obey the straight and narrow pathway to success: job specialization.
10. Thou shalt have an answer to all problems at all times.[3]

As I have conducted marriage enrichment seminars with thousands of couples across the country over the past ten years, many wives have shared the same concern: "Men do not share their emotions sufficiently." These women say they do not know what their husbands are feeling or if they are feeling. The husbands avoid being known. (This appears to be true in their relationships with other men as well as women. See David Smith's excellent book *The Friendless American Male,* Regal Books.)

Many men do not have a sufficient vocabulary to express their emotions. As they were learning to be men they learned to value expressions of masculinity and to devalue what they labeled "feminine" expressions. These men are locked up emotionally. They are not comfortable sharing their failures, anxieties or disappointments. An indicator of being a man is "I can do it by myself. I don't need any help." Unfortunately this leads to the inability to say "help me" when help is desperately needed. Masculinity means not depending on anybody. Dependence is equated with being a parasite. These men resist being dependent. This often shows up in the man's obsession with his work, his inability to relax and play—unless he is in a highly competitive situation, and his struggle with weekends and vacations.

Many men think that all feelings are "weaknesses." Sympathy and empathy are awkward for them. Fear is one of the most difficult emotions for them to admit.

Some men (and some women) use their intellect to defend against their feelings. They may dissect, analyze, and discuss their emotions, but they do not spontaneously share them. Men and women have the same emotions. Men do NOT have different emotions than women. We simply differ in our expression of them. Many men are seen as totally cognitive or logical. Many women are seen as totally relational and feeling oriented. Could it be that we are actually both? Could it be that there are various forms of logic? Not everyone goes directly from *A* to *B* to *C*. Some leave *A* and make several side trips before coming back to *B* and then take several other side trips before arriving at *C*. Some go through this process in a few short words, others add descriptive adjectives and paint a beautiful mental picture. Consider Dr. Ross Campbell's discussion of the difference between emotional and factual communication.

> We can start by realizing that there is a difference between cognitive (that is, intellectual or rational) communications and emotional (that is, feeling) communications. Persons who communicate primarily on a cognitive level deal mainly with factual data. They like to talk about such topics as sports, the stock market, money, houses, jobs, etc., keeping the subject of conversation out of the emotional area. Usually they are quite uncomfortable dealing with issues which elicit feelings, especially unpleasant feelings such as anger. Consequently, they avoid talking

about subjects which involve love, fear, and anger. These persons have difficulty, then, being warm and supportive of their spouses.

Others communicate more on the feeling level. They tire easily of purely factual data, and feel a need to share feelings, specially with their spouses. They feel the atmosphere between husband and wife must be as free as possible from unpleasant feelings like tension, anger, and resentment. So, of course, they want to talk about these emotional things, resolve conflicts with their spouse, clear the air, and keep things pleasant between them.

Of course no one is completely cognitive or completely emotional.

/_____/_____/_____/_____/_____/_____/_____/_____/_____/

Emotional   Cognitive

1. Indicate where you are on this graph by placing your initials near the appropriate mark.

2. Indicate where each of your family members is on the chart, using their initials.

3. Indicate where you think they would place you on the chart. Mark your initials and circle them . . . .

A person on the left side of the graph, who shares more feelings, is not less bright or less intellectual. This person is simply aware of his/her feelings and is usually better able to do something about them. On the other hand, a person on the right side of the graph, who displays less feelings, does not have less feelings; the feelings are simply suppressed and buried, and this person is less aware and often blind to his feelings.

A surprising fact is that the so-called cognitive person (on the right) is controlled by his feelings just as is the so-called emotional person but he doesn't realize it. For example, the stiff, formal intellectual has deep feelings also, but uses enormous energy to keep them buried so he won't be bothered with them. But unfortunately they do bother him. Whenever someone (like an "emotional" wife, or child) is around asking him for affection and warmth, he is not only unable to respond, he is angered that his precious equilibrium has been disturbed.[4]

One belief which some men hold is that being masculine automatically means being logical, analytical, or scientific. The word *logical* means "capable of reasoning or of using reason in an orderly cogent fashion." Therefore intuition or the ability to sense or feel what is happening is not available to many men, for that seems feminine. They believe that logic and intuition cannot work together.

Warren Farrell raises an interesting question: "Must a person who expresses emotions think without logic or does it ultimately free one to think logically?"[5] Isn't it possible that a person who is in touch with his emotions and expresses them freely may see things accurately and make decisions logically and perceptively as well? Feelings are not to be feared but experienced and expressed. They are to be accepted as one of God's gifts and used to add greater depth to life. Feelings are to be used as an inner release.

Herb Goldberg, in his enlightening book *The Hazards of Being Male,* describes the destructive consequences for a man who does not express his emotions.

1. He is vulnerable to sudden, unpredictable behavior.

2. He denies his feelings and needs and then becomes resentful because intimates take him at face value and don't read his hidden self correctly.

3. He becomes prone to emotional upsets and disturbances.

4. He becomes prone to countless psychophysiological disorders.

5. The defenses against feeling force him further and further away from relationships.

6. His inability to ask for help means that when his defenses begin to shatter, he begins to withdraw further or turns to drugs or alcohol.[6]

contributions to a male mid-life crisis (See *Seasons of a Marriage* for a complete discussion). A man was not created to deny his emotions. No one was. Neither were we created to just express our emotions and not use the cognitive ability God has given us. Some people's communication reflects a life devoid of correct thinking and feeling.

In His creative act God has given all of us different temperaments, talents, spiritual gifts, skills, and motivations. Our culture and upbringing, however, can create a filter which keeps us from experiencing our full creation. Soon we begin to be molded to this world. But Paul tells us, "Do not be conformed to this world, but be transformed by the renewing of your mind, that you may prove what the will of God is, that which is good and acceptable and perfect" (Rom. 12:2).

Even if women are more prone to express their emotions and empathy, does the Word of God say that this is the way it was meant to be? Culture might tell us that emotions are female traits, but God's Word does not agree. Jesus expressed anger. He wept. He felt distress and was deeply depressed! In the Word of God we are called to experience various attitudes and demonstrate outward expressions of Christian growth and character. In the Sermon on the Mount Jesus says blessed are those who are sorrowful, who possess a gentle spirit, who show mercy, whose hearts are pure, and who are peaceful. We are called to manifest the fruit of the Spirit which is love, joy, peace, patience, kindness, goodness, faithfulness, gentleness, and self-control.

Jack Balswick, a Ph.D. in sociology, argues that the strongest evidence that innate temperamental differences exist with each sex is the general similarity of behavior for males and females in most cultures. While the sexes differ in physiology and in temperament, much of what we call male or female behavior or attitudes is social conditioning (nurture) rather than the result of biology (nature). Much behavior that is now explained as biologically either male or female may just as easily be explained by social conditioning.[7]

If we have learned certain patterns of behavior in the past, the good news is that we can also unlearn them and begin to respond in a new way. The result will be a change for the better in our ability to communicate.

Look back at the original list of items which were purported to be differences between men and women. Words like *always* or *never* are too absolute. They simply perpetuate a stereotype.

What Do You Think?

1. Do any of those statements describe you? If so, how do you feel about this *tendency* in your life?

2. How does this tendency affect your marriage? Specifically, the communication process?

3. Is this a tendency that you would like to change? If so, why?

4. How does your spouse feel about this tendency?

You may find that your own tendencies do not fit what has been suggested as a female or male characteristic.

BUILD YOUR VOCABULARY

If you do not know how to share your feelings and emotions, obtain a synonym finder or thesaurus and begin to expand your vocabulary. When it comes time to share, give three or four descriptive sentences instead of a one-line summary. Your description should include at least one feeling or emotional word.

I mention the one-line summary because in the groups of

married couples I mentioned earlier a major complaint of the women is: "Men never give sufficient details. They give us the summary." As one woman expressed it, "Jim is on the phone for twenty minutes talking to a friend. When he gets off and I ask him what they said, he gives me a one-line summation. I don't want the condensed version. I want the whole novel-length story! One day he came home and told me he had just run into one of our closest friends and the man's wife had had their baby early that morning. I asked him, 'Well, was it a boy or girl? How large was it? What time was it born? etc.' He said all he remembered is that they had their baby. He didn't remember all those trivial details!"

Another woman in a seminar suggested that "men tend to view communication like a telegram. Women view it as a meal to be savored." Men tend not to share many details in certain areas or about certain topics. But listen to us as we talk about what is important to *us*! Our work, our hobbies, our recreation, etc. Men can be just as detailed and precise as anyone else when they want to. And they can express themselves in detail with emotion as well. I have heard the communication of men that has moved me to tears. Each year I read dozens of novels and many of the authors are men. They paint word pictures in my mind that are a combination of facts, feelings, and descriptive adjectives. We *are* capable.

A man who is more of a cognitive responder not only can build his vocabulary, he can begin to think out loud in the presence of his wife. He can say to her, "I'm going to just brainstorm out loud and what I say may not make complete sense or have continuity but I'm willing to try and describe my day differently for you." And as he does this his wife has the opportunity to listen and take in. She should not criticize, correct, or make any value judgments about what he is saying.

A simple way to learn how to expand what we say is the *XYZ* method: X is the actual event you want to describe; Y are your feelings about the event; Z are the consequences or results of the event.

Instead of coming home from work and saying, "I bought a new car today." Period. Try expanding on the topic: "Guess

what I did. Boy, am I excited! I finally did something I've always wanted to do but was afraid to. I saw this new car on the lot that was just what we'd talked about three months ago. I saw the price, offered them $400 less, and bought it. I feel great. In fact I feel like a kid again, and it's a car we can afford! How would you like to take a ride with me tonight?"

Remember to share more than the event. People who care about you want to know your inner feelings as well as your thinking. If you make a decision about something, don't just share the decision. Share with your spouse the process that led you to make that decision.

What can a wife do to help her husband share his feelings?

A wife can do a number of things to help her husband become more expressive, but the changes, if they do occur, will take time. You are battling years of conditioning, so beware of making demands that he can't meet as yet.

Barbara, a forty-year-old mother and accountant, said, "When I wanted John to share, I wanted his feelings when I wanted them. My requests came across as demands. And one day he told me so. I learned to be sensitive to his days and moods and whenever he began to share some of his frustrations I listened and listened well. He didn't want a dialogue or someone to solve his problem. He wanted to vent, and I wanted to hear!"

Some of the suggestions that follow may sound familiar, others quite new. Remember, if what you're doing now isn't working, why keep using the same approach? A new approach used in a loving, consistent manner may help build the intimacy you're looking for.

Help your husband acknowledge that he has feelings inside of him, and that by learning to share these the relationship will bloom. One husband said, "After fifteen years of marriage, I wondered why our relationship was so stale. And then I realized it wasn't the relationship, it was me! When Jan asked me questions or wanted to talk, I gave her thoughts and facts, but no feelings. She could have gotten the same from a computer. We decided to take fifteen minutes a day to share. She agreed to summarize her three-minute descriptions into three or four lines. I agreed to share whatever I said with feeling words. It took us a while to learn this new style, but what a difference it has made! I share—she listens—and we feel closer."

Try direct questions that encourage a direct response.

"I'd like to know the most interesting experience you had at work today (or this week)."

"When have you felt angry, sad, excited, happy, or whatever this week and what caused it?"

"I feel there's a portion of you I don't know. If I had to describe how you feel about your work, what would I say?"

"You really seem to enjoy your woodworking. What do you enjoy so much about it?"

"When you were a little boy, what were your greatest delights and your greatest fears?"

By asking thought-provoking questions about topics fairly comfortable to him—like work, hobby, childhood—you make it easier for him to communicate. These questions vary in their degree of comfort. Sometimes it's easier to pose a factual question first, then lead into how he feels about it. Most husbands find it easy to describe facts about work. But it may take them time to discuss the joys, frustrations, or boredom of their job.

One wife asked her husband: "Honey, you know I enjoy hearing more details and feelings from you. Often it appears that you seem hesitant to talk to me about them. Is there something I do to make it difficult for you to share these with me?"

Another wife was more direct: "John, you know I like to hear the details, your feelings, the inner workings of who you are. I need this, and the times you have shared with me were fantastic. You're so articulate and have such depth. You probably feel I pressure you, or even nag you, into opening up to me. I know you don't like it when I do slip into that trap. I want you to know that I'm not trying to nag. But I do appreciate your sharing more with me."

Develop an atmosphere of trust so he will eventually be able to express the entire gamut of feeling arising in him. If you ask your husband how he feels about his job and he says he hates it and wants to quit, your own feelings of insecurity may cause you to respond, "You can't! Think of us and our children!" And your husband won't be as open with you again. You don't have to agree with his feelings; the goal is not to debate, but to build communication and thus intimacy.

Thank him for sharing. Let your husband know how much it means to you and ask if there's anything you can do to make it easier for him. Before he leaves for work in the morning ask what it is that you can pray about for him that day. This gives you something specific to talk about at the end of the day.

Often watching a movie together can open the emotional side of a person. A film can bring out feelings in a person who would ordinarily suppress them. Emotions brought to the surface through the film seem "safe" because in a sense they are not "real." Discussing the movie later, using factual and feeling questions, may lead to a unique discussion.

What then is the answer to some of the complaints and concerns which men and women bring up about one another? The answer is, *adjust, change,* and *reinforce* any changes which occur.

Let's look once again at some of the items of the original list of male/female differences. But note the changes which are more accurate. Some of the statements have been combined.

1. Men and women may be a bit different in the way they communicate and relate to others. These differences, if quite strong, can be complementary and they can change.

2. Both men and women think and feel internally. Men tend to verbalize thoughts and ideas whereas women tend to express emotions and feelings more than men.

3. Language spoken and heard for some men and women may be either an emotional experience or a thinking experience. But how would you know? You really wouldn't unless you asked questions and discussed it with your spouse. What about you? What kind of an experience is it for you? Have you shared this with your spouse?

4. Men or women may tend to take statements personally or impersonally. You might not know because they may keep it hidden inside. If you think your partner tends to take situations or statements personally, check it out with him—ask and discuss. If he does take something personally, could it be because

of something you have said.

5. In material or spiritual matters, it varies with the individual whether he/she is more concerned with the ultimate or the process of getting there.

6. Are men like filing cabinets and women like computers? Could it be that the difference is really in how much we verbalize? How we deal with problems may be due to two important factors discussed earlier in this book: the resolution of past issues, and our self talk.

7. For many women her home is an extension of her personality, but so is her work. For most men their job is not only an extension of their personality but the source of their identity.

8. All men and women have a need for security and roots. Perhaps women express this need more. For many homemakers their home is the source of security and rootedness. Men may appear to be nomadic if a job change occurs because their work has such a high degree of significance for them. Thus to another person they appear not to care about the roots of the home and family. Many men say that the fact that they do love and care for their family is the reason they strive to get ahead in their job and take advancement opportunities.

9. Both men and women have a wide variety of emotions available to them. Some individuals become tied into experiencing one emotion more than others because they reinforce its occurrence. A person becomes used to expressing anger, fear, or sorrow.

10. Women are not always changing and men are not the stable sex per se. A man or woman can be either. Often we tend to evaluate people on the basis of their verbal expressions and are led to believe in a stereotyped view. Those who are impulsive with few inner controls—whether men or women—are the ones who become too involved too soon.

11. We tend to remember what is most important to us. Some events and items hold greater significance than others. If we can remember details at work we can learn to remember details at home or socially if we choose to do so. There are also times when the details of an event are just not that important to us, and that's all right! We need to discuss why some details are

so important to a person in order to understand his perspective. Distortions occur because a topic or event is not that important to the speaker or the listener. We may not have been listening, we don't understand our past, or our self talk is interfering with our current communication.

What Do You Think?

1. Write a paragraph describing how your mother communicated, how your father communicated, and in what way you are like them.

2. Ask your spouse to describe how you communicate.

3. What specific changes will you make this week in your communication with your spouse?

Notes
1. David Smith, *The Friendless American Male* (Ventura, CA: Regal Books, 1983), p. 37.
2. Ibid., p. 43.
3. Warren Farrell, *The Liberated Man* (New York: Random House, Inc., 1974).
4. Ross Campbell, *How to Really Love Your Child* (Wheaton, IL: Scripture Press Publications, 1977), pp. 19-20.
5. Farrell, *The Liberated Man*, pp. 328-329.
6. Herb Goldberg, *The Hazards of Being Male* (New York: The New American Library, 1975), p. 39.
7. Smith, *Friendless American Male*, p. 48.

CHAPTER 8

DO YOU REALLY WANT YOUR SPOUSE TO CHANGE?

We are strange creatures. For years we search for just the right person to be our mate—someone who is attractive, loving, considerate, and all those other qualities we hold dear. At last we find the right one and we hasten to tie the knot. Then are we satisfied? Not exactly. Our reforming tendencies soon emerge and the struggle begins. Our mate may not *want* to change, and, if the truth were known, he or she would like *us* to change![1]

Are we abnormal in wanting to change another person? Do all couples desire change in their relationship and their partner? Yes, indeed. The desire for change is a natural response when we are committed to another person. Too often couples do not realize that desiring change in each other is an act of caring.

The question before us, however, is: Am I willing to change as much as I want my partner to change? Perhaps God is asking *you* to be a pacesetter in change as an example to others, for your own benefit and for the glory of God. Look at what Scripture says to each of us. We are called to be people who change! "Not that I have now attained [this ideal] or am already made perfect, but I press on to lay hold of (grasp) and make my own, that for which Christ Jesus, the Messiah, has laid hold of me and made me His Own. I do not consider, brethren, that I have captured and made it my own [yet]; but one thing I do—it is my one aspiration: forgetting what lies behind and straining forward to what lies ahead, I press on toward the goal to win the [supreme and heavenly] prize to which God in Christ Jesus is calling us upward" (Phil. 3:12-14, *AMP*).

"Like newborn babies you should crave—thirst for, earnestly desire—the pure (unadulterated) spiritual milk, that by it you may be nurtured and grow into [completed] salvation" (1 Pet. 2:2, *AMP*).

But what about trying to change others? Isn't that wrong? Isn't it unethical or selfish to expect another person to change his actions or his attitude? Too often we adopt a hands-off philosophy and assume a pious spirituality. "I will accept my spouse exactly as he or she is and not make any attempt to change him," we say. Or "I just want to change the relationship, not the other person." If you take this attitude, why do you read books on marriage and communication such as this one! Our desire to change is seen in the vast multitude of marriage books published in the last decade. Look at the thousands of people who attend Marriage Enrichment Seminars! If people didn't want to change themselves and their mates, why invest all this money, time, and energy? "But I just want to *improve* my marriage," you reply. That's fine, but improvement necessitates change on someone's part.

So what is our response as a married person to be? Total blind acceptance of our spouse and our marriage as it is? Or could God use us as a positive factor to bring about change?

We are called upon to be enablers or encouragers. Would a

desire to bring about change fit the role of being an enabler or encourager? *If we were to evaluate the desired change in light of the Scripture would we discover that this change we are called to make is from the Word of God?*

What is it you want to change in your relationship? Is it something specific or something general? Is it an attitude or behavior? Usually we want our spouse to change his or her attitude. It is easier for people to change their behavior, however, than their attitude. If a change actually occurs, all you will see is a change in behavior. That change in behavior may or may not reflect a genuine change in attitude.

What happens when we honestly want change but feel that we should not or cannot do anything to make it happen? We learn to cope. But there is a cost to coping. Too often we do not anticipate this cost and its effect upon our own life and the relationship. There are several ways to cope, some active and some passive.

PASSIVE COPING

There are two passive ways to cope—resignation and martyrdom.

Resignation: "I give up," Joan says. "I just have to accept the fact that Jimmy is always going to leave his clothes all over the house. I haven't found any way to change his sloppy habits, and now other people are telling me I just need to accept him as he is. I'm going to have to learn to live with the fact that I'll always have to pick up after my husband."

The acceptance which we see here in Joan is coming from a feeling of impotence. "I'm stuck and I better learn to live with it." When we resign ourselves to accepting another person's undesirable behavior, we admit that we are powerless. Soon this begins to erode our sense of self-esteem. And when you start thinking less of yourself, how do you think that affects your view of your spouse? You're right! You begin to think less of him or her also. You begin to care less for the person and you may begin to withdraw. Resignation can be destructive in a relationship. Soon you will begin to feel a sense of loss for what the relationship could have been.

Martyrdom: A martyr accepts the behavior of others that he feels he is unable to change. But he uses this acceptance to show others how good *he* is. He frequently reminds his mate (and other people as well) of the sacrifice he is making in putting up with his mate's behavior. This becomes a sore spot in the relationship and the mate learns to tune the martyr out. The martyr in turn withdraws and in time begins to question the relationship itself.

ACTIVE COPING

There are also two rather active responses to our inability to bring about change.

Revenge: We proclaim "Vengeance is mine" in small insignificant ways which may go unnoticed at first. A spouse who is tightly controlled and dominated by his/her partner may begin to lie about his/her activities when on his/her own. A spouse who is restricted financially by the frugality of the other partner may use some of the budgeted money secretly for his/her own use. Other responses are more than obvious and quite direct. Revenge is a subtle response against both our spouse and our marriage. It stems from our anger over not being able to change the relationship. But revenge is counterproductive. Does it bring about the change we desire? Does it move us closer to our mate? Not likely. Our expressions of revenge may bring about the very same response in our mate.

Withdrawal: This is a declaration that "if I can't change you, then I choose not to be involved with you at all!" There are degrees of withdrawal ranging from the most extreme of divorce or separation to living together as "married singles" sharing only the same house. Caring, love, and commitment become foreigners in a land of pretense for the sake of others. Couples pay a great price of emotional hurt in a "withdrawal within a relationship." Withdrawal is a costly option.

What Do You Think?

Listed below are the four typical coping responses we have just discussed. Think back to the home in which you were raised. Indicate which of these (if any) were modeled for you in your parents' relationship. Then indicate the result.

Coping response   *Result*

1. Resignation

2. Martyrdom

3. Revenge

4. Withdrawal

Now indicate which responses you have used with your own mate in different (or maybe the same) situations. Indicate the consequences and then how you felt afterwards.

Situations   *How I Coped*   *Consequences*   *My Feelings*

How do you now respond when change does not occur?

What are some of the reasons we want other people to change? The usual ones are: "I don't like what he/she does." "It creates more work for me." "It's for his own good." "I have to complete the work his parents never finished." "I just want to improve our relationship."

Are these really the reasons? No, they are not. Are the changes for the person's own good? Are the changes really for the good of the relationship? Or are they for *our* own good? What is the reason?

REAL REASONS WE WANT CHANGE

Here are some of the *real* reasons that lie behind our desire for change. They may surprise you! Underlying all of these reasons is our need to belong, to be accepted, to be loved, to feel we are special to another person.

We seek renewal. Sometimes we lose the feelings of affirmation we originally had, thus we ask for a change in the relationship to renew those positive feelings we once experienced in our relationship. We want to recapture good feelings about ourselves, and we want our spouse to change in some way so things can again "be the way they once were." We want renewal. A wife may want to recapture the first year of marriage. "I want him to take the afternoon off once a week as he did twenty years ago. We would go for a walk or ride bikes or lie on the floor in front of the fireplace and read or talk. I guess I want him to court me again."

We want more. We may feel that we have not received sufficient affirmation of our self-image and we want more. Our need for positive input from others will vary according to events and circumstances and our own individual development. When we want more it may mean quality or a different approach. "My husband is attractive. He touches me, compliments me now and then, but often I hint for the compliments. I would like him to think for himself and create new compliments. I want to be loved and pursued ten times the amount I am now. In fact, I'd settle for a 50 percent increase! And I don't want to tell him how to do it either!"

We need variety. A different expression of affirmation is needed if we feel our spouse has taken us for granted or our relationship has become routine. If our partner affirms us in the same old ways, it is not enough. His or her love and concern needs to be expressed in some new way so we are convinced of our spouse's sincerity. "My wife is very loving and affirming. But she is so predictable. I like all that she does but it's almost like she's been programmed a certain way. I want some surprises. I'd like her to say new things to me, to be different in her sexual responses too. I guess I should be satisfied. So many men don't receive what I do, and yet . . . "

We want to be seen in a different light. We also want our partner to affirm us for more than one aspect of who we are. One
woman said, "I want to be seen not just as a competent home-
maker. I'd like my husband to see that I have value as a teacher,
as a creative thinker, but he can't seem to grasp that." New affirmation gives us the feeling of being even more valued and special. Concern for the other person and the relationship may be
tied in to all of these other reasons.

These are only four reasons people seek change. There are
others. Some very insecure people cannot tolerate different-
ness. Others have a need to dominate and must be in control of
change.

How does the biblical mandate to exhort one another or
encourage one another apply to the marriage relationship? The
Word of God gives us examples of our response to one another
(italics have been added).

"And when [Apollos] wished to cross to Achaia [most of
Greece], the brethren wrote to the disciples there, *urging* and
encouraging them to accept and welcome him heartily" (Acts
18:27, *AMP*).

"I *entreat* and *advise* Euodia and I entreat and advise Syn-
tyche to agree and to work in harmony in the Lord" (Phil. 4:2,
AMP).

"Let the word [spoken by] the Christ, the Messiah, have its
home (in your hearts and minds) and dwell in you in [all its] rich-
ness, as you *teach* and *admonish* and *train one* another in all
insight and intelligence and wisdom [in spiritual things, and sing]
psalms and hymns and spiritual songs, making melody to God
with [His] grace in your hearts" (Col. 3:16, *AMP*).

"But we beseech and earnestly exhort you, brethren, that
you excel (in this matter) more and more" (1 Thess. 4:10,
AMP).

"Therefore encourage (admonish, exhort) one another and
edify—strengthen and build up—one another, just as you are
doing" (1 Thess. 5:11, *AMP*).

Who determines what we are to exhort another person to
do? Who determines what we are to teach another or encourage
another person to do?

The word *exhort* in these passages means to urge one to pursue some course of conduct. It is always looking to the future. Exhorting one another is a three-fold ministry in which a believer urges another to action in terms of applying scriptural truth, encourages the other with scriptural truth and comforts the other through the application of Scripture. *Encourage* is to urge forward or persuade in Acts 18:27. In 1 Thessalonians 5:11 it means to stimulate another to the ordinary duties of life. Therefore, what are we to exhort another person to do?

To answer this you need to look at your motives for change. When you begin to understand what your motives really are, you may discover that it isn't really necessary for your spouse to change. Perhaps your needs can be fulfilled in other ways which allow your partner not to have to change. If you can discover why you want your spouse to change, you may discover what you want change in your own life. The key is to understand your own motives.

What Do You Think?

Indicate any changes you would like your spouse to make. Select the reason from the "Real Reasons We Want Change."

Changes   *Reason*

A STRATEGY FOR CHANGE

When you ask your spouse to change some behavior of his/hers that you do not like, he/she will interpret the proposed change in one of four ways: (1) as a destructive change; (2) as a threatening change; (3) as having no effect upon him/her; or (4) as a change that would help him/her become a better person. Thus it is important in requesting a change to present the suggestion in such a way that your spouse sees it as an opportunity for growth. How can this be done?

First of all, *you must give him information.* Each person has a different need for and capacity for handling information. For most individuals, the more information you provide about a desired change the less the resistance. Why? Because there is more opportunity for him to see the request for change as a step toward growth. "John, I appreciate your interest in the children and their education. I'd like you to help me in two areas with them—David needs your assistance with some of his projects and I need your help in talking to his teacher. I understand that this may take some time, but your opinions and knowledge can help David more than I can. If we both talk to the teacher we'll both be able to share our ideas and also present a united front to both the teacher and David." A person needs to know what you expect of him, why you expect it, and what may be the results.

Involving your partner in exploring various alternatives for change will also lessen resistance. Your spouse will be less defensive if he/she has a chance to express his/her ideas and make suggestions. "Jan, you know that we've been able to talk a bit more lately about how the home is kept and also our scheduling difficulties. I'm wondering if we could explore some possible alternatives that might work. This doesn't mean we're going to just accept whatever idea is shared, but just that we get some more ideas to work with. What do you think?"

Start out slowly so that it's easier to do. Is the change requested an overwhelming and gigantic step? Or have you broken the request down into small increments which can actually be accomplished? If so, there may be a better response. If the requested change is for increased communication, starting out sharing for fifteen minutes one night a week is reasonable. The goal may be thirty minutes a night, four nights a week, but that is too much to expect at first. Having the garage cleaned and kept clean is a typical request. But developing a specific small-step plan to accomplish this over a four-month period of time may be workable.

Intimacy is a final factor. Resistance is a normal response when one partner mistrusts and fears the other. If motives or intentions are questioned, how can a suggested change be seen as anything but damaging? If trust and intimacy exist, a spouse may see the request as one way to achieve even greater intimacy in the marriage. A wife who has responded favorably to her husband's previous suggestions for change will be open if:

1. Her husband acknowledges her change in a positive way. He doesn't say, "Well, it won't last," or "It's about time," or "I can't believe it."

2. He doesn't mention her change or lack of change in front of others to embarrass her.

3. He is open to changes himself.

4. She knows he loves her whether she changes or not.

5. She sees his request for change as something that will enhance her life.

RESISTANCE TO CHANGE

Why do we resist change? Why is it difficult to comply with the requests of others? Too often the reasons we give are covers for the real source of resistance.

If a spouse doesn't respond positively to a request to change, his resistance can take many forms.

Some people simply stop listening as an expression of their unwillingness to change. They cut off the conversation, leave the room, or busy themselves with some task. A man may stay late at the office or a woman may say she has to leave early for an appointment in order to prevent further discussion.

On the other hand, some people agree with the request, but *they do not follow through on it* because they have no intention of doing so. This is a stall tactic to get the person making the request to back off! But after numerous requests with no follow-through, the spouse becomes suspicious and angry.

Or perhaps the person counters with, "Why don't *you* change?" a resistance tactic which *throws the request back to the person making it*. This completely turns the request around and the result will probably be an argument.

Why are we so reluctant to change?

One simple reason for not changing is habit. Day in and day out we maintain a fairly predictable routine. Inside of us we have a selection of comfortable responses which make us feel secure. We don't have to think about or work at new ways of responding. But the habits that make us feel secure may be an irritant to others. Habit is probably the most frequently used form of resistance. Why? Because it works so well.

Have you ever used these excuses or heard them used? "I've always done it this way." "After twenty-eight years, it's too late to change now." "Why change? I'm comfortable. This way works." "How do I know the new way is better? I don't have to think about this one. I just do it."

Perhaps you live with someone who is messy. The person does not: pick up after himself; put items away; hang up his clothes when he comes home from work; change into old clothes before he does a messy chore; pick up the paper and magazines he dropped on the floor; clear his own dishes away from the table.

You may have tried to correct this individual by begging, pleading, threatening, letting the mess accumulate for days or even weeks, but nothing has worked. Probably your mate was accustomed to having people pick up after him while he was growing up. If this is the case, perhaps he developed the belief that he is special and deserves to be waited on. If he was waited on and picked up after for many years and now his spouse is saying, "Pick up after yourself," the message he is receiving is, "You no longer deserve to be catered to." Thus his self-esteem is under attack. The way he thinks about himself has been challenged. This is the real reason why he resists. If he changes he will have to change some perceptions he holds about himself.

Habits can be changed. A habit of twenty-five years can change as quickly as one of ten years or one year once the source of resistance is discovered. And the change is easier than most people realize.

There are others who plead ignorance as their resistance. "I didn't know that's what you wanted"; "I don't know how to do that. What do you think you married? Superman?" Ignorance can be an effective tool because it puts the person making the request on the defensive. He begins to question whether he *did* tell his mate what he wanted or whether he is expecting too much.

Control is another resistance frequently used. If someone asks me to change I may not comply because of my fear of losing control. I want to stay in control of me and even you. The resistance to change comes about because of what that change would communicate about who is in control of the situation. We don't like others determining how we are to behave. The request may not be a control issue but we interpret it in that manner.

Uncertainty or anxiety is an honest resistance response. "How will this change affect me?" "Will I be capable?" "Will people still respond to me in the same way?" "What if I can't do it to please you?" We anticipate some threats and fears coming into play. *We feel our self-esteem being challenged and threatened, and this again is the key: Any perceived threat to our self-esteem is going to be resisted. Will I still receive affirmation? Will I be as secure?*

Do you really think that all your requests for change should meet with instant applause and compliance? If your partner resists your request for change do you become angry, despondent, perplexed, stubborn? Can you see value in resistance? Probably not. But consider the possibilities.

If your requests are resisted, perhaps this will cause you to consider why you want the change, how intensely you want it, and how committed you are to pursuing the change. What does your commitment level to this change tell you about your own needs at this time?

Perhaps the resistance will assist you in being more specific concerning what it is you wish changed. Have you considered your mate's resistance as a unique form of communication? He could be telling you something new about himself—what he values, what elements are involved in his self-esteem. If the person's resistance is too strong, you may be convinced to try another approach.

HOW TO PROMOTE CHANGE

How can we motivate others to change? We have been told for years that we cannot change others, only they can change themselves. That's true. But how can we help to create the conditions under which another person would desire to change? Let's look at the main means which are used to bring about change.

First of all, here are several ineffective but frequently used means of bringing about change.

The first of these is the show me tactic: "If you loved me you would . . . " Have you ever been asked to change as a demonstration of your love for your mate? Have you ever asked your mate to change for this reason? The response we usually get or give is: "If you loved me, you wouldn't ask!"

Next, some try to trade off: "Look I'll change _____ if you'll change _____ ." This is like saying, "I've got a deal for you!"

Frequently people resort to the demand: "You better do this or else I will . . . " This is a risky approach and can backfire. It also sounds like power play.

For centuries people have used power and coercion to bring about change. Threats, demands, and rewards are frequently used, including giving or withholding verbal or physical affection, and even abuse. Power can work, but what are the consequences? None of us likes to be dominated by another person.

Another approach is to make people worry, feel uncomfortable, or ill at ease about what they do. If we can create guilt or anxiety we think we can bring about change. But the change is usually not real or lasting. Instead of bringing about the change we seek, the other person may actually withdraw from us. We don't like to be around people who make us feel uncomfortable. It is difficult to develop intimacy between people when either power or discomfort is used as a means of bringing about change.

But there are legitimate and effective methods that can be used to promote change. *One approach is to provide new information* that will help the other person move to a new behavior. This approach is based upon believing that our mate will examine new data and make a rational decision to change. Hopefully the person will discover that what he is currently doing will not achieve his goals as well as using the new approach. The information approach may be effective, but it is quite slow. The person must clearly see the consequences of the new suggestion and the ways it will enhance his feelings of self-worth.

Another approach is called the growth approach. If the person can see little or no risk involved to himself and his self-image, he may be open to change. "If I don't have anything to lose, I may try it." The key is to eliminate risk! Which means the person

needs to be assured that his self-image will remain intact or even be enhanced. This is the ideal. There will always be some degree of risk however.

Of all strategies for change *the most intimate is trust.* Trust is paramount if you wish to bring about change. If you have a solid basis of trust already established, your requests may find a response. If there is no pattern of trust, it may take a while to build it. And if trust has been destroyed you may never rebuild it. Trust and credibility (yours!) are at stake.

To build trust, and to request change based on this trust, requests for change should be very simple and trivial to begin with. Think of how safe the other person feels now. How safe and secure will he need to feel before he responds to your request?

If your mate is going to change he must see that you are trustworthy and that you seek the best for him. And all you can do is *request* change. It is up to the other person to *decide* to change and do it. Before you begin, are the changes you request in harmony with the pattern of living as stated in Scripture? Or do the changes reflect your own insecurities? Remember, "We try to change people to conform to our ideas of how they should be. So does God. But there the similarity ends. Our ideas of what the other person should do or how he should act may be an improvement or an imprisonment. We may be setting the other person free of behavior patterns that are restricting his development, or we may be simply chaining him up in another behavioral bondage."[2]

Change can occur if *you* will do the following:

1. Examine and clarify your reasons and desires for change. Examine your need.

2. Evaluate the requests in light of Scripture. Is this a change which Scripture calls upon us to make?

3. Understand how your partner sees him/herself and what his/her self-esteem is built upon.

4. Present changes in a way that enhances his/her self-esteem.

5. Consider your own willingness to change. Are you willing to stand by your mate and encourage, edify, and build him/her

up? Are you open to change and is that openness obvious to others? A yes answer to these questions is vital.

6. Reinforce, reinforce, and reinforce! If your mate makes a requested change and you ignore it or take it for granted, he/she will feel violated, let down, and will revert back to his/her previous behavior. We all need feedback and reward for making a change. Then our self-esteem remains intact. Changes are fragile and must be strengthened. When I *experience* affirmation as a person for my new behavior I feel like making it a part and parcel of my life-style. If I feel uncertain with this new behavior, then I will return to the certainty of the old. And the new experience and reinforcement needs to be strong. Otherwise, I remember my old experience which is a natural part of my life and is not easily overcome. The reinforcement must come at a time when it can be linked to the new behavior. This means right after it occurs.

7. Be persistent and patient. Don't expect too much too soon and don't become a defeatist.

What Do You Think?

1. List a change you would like to see in your relationship with your spouse.

2. What changes would you like your spouse to make and what changes will you make?

3. In what way is your spouse's current behavior tied into his self-esteem?

4. Describe how you will present your request so that your partner will feel that this is going to enhance his self-esteem.

Notes

1. Many of the concepts in this chapter came from Michael E. McGill, *Changing Him, Changing Her* (New York: Simon & Schuster, 1982).
2. James G. T. Fairfield, *When You Don't Agree* (Scottdale, PA: Herald Press, 1977.

CHAPTER 9

ANGER AND COMMUNICATION

Who makes you angry? You do! Situations and other people cannot make you angry. No matter what your spouse does, he or she does not make you angry. You create your own anger.

Anger, like other emotions, is created by your own thoughts. If your spouse fails to follow through with a commitment he has made to you, you may become angry. Your anger comes from your thoughts about the meaning or significance you have given to his failure to follow through.

WHAT CREATES ANGER?

There are many ways we create our own anger. But we do create our own anger. We may label our partner in some way because of what he has or has not done by thinking (or even verbalizing): "You jerk"; "You selfish person"; "You inconsiderate clown." We label a person in anger because of something he/she has done. But in doing so we tear him/her down. His/her good points are discounted. All you see is this one event and any others similar to it, passing over the things you love about him/her.

Sometimes we become angry when our self-esteem is threatened. Perhaps your spouse insulted or criticized you. You may not feel loved or liked and that feeling makes you angry.

Anger can also be generated by mind reading. In your mind you create your own reasons for why your spouse did what he or she did and you project those reasons onto him.

"That's his mean nature. He's just like his father."

"She just wants to argue for the heck of it."

"Anyone who acts like that must not have any love or compassion."

But mind reading never works. You cannot know for certain the thoughts and motivation of another person. Mind reading only creates additional conflicts.

Inappropriate should/shouldn't statements create highly flammable fuel for your anger. Whenever you say, "My spouse shouldn't (or should) have done that" you create the setting for anger. What you are doing is interpreting a situation a certain way and saying it should have been different. When you insist on holding onto the "shoulds," you keep yourself festered and upset. It would have been nice if the other person had performed as you wanted, but he didn't. Your anger won't change the past and probably will do little to alter the future. Consider the following two situations:

Situation 1: The house is a mess. Especially the kitchen. John's wife is gone and he decides he is going to treat his wife by cleaning the living room, family room, and kitchen. He vacuums, sweeps, dusts and washes dishes for two hours. "Wait until she sees this. Will she be surprised! She'll go wild with appreciation." So he hopes.

Sometime later his wife, Janice, arrives home with bags of groceries and clothes. She staggers into the house and drops the bags in the living room.

"John, would you bring in some of the groceries for me please? There are so many and I'm beat. Wait until you see the great prices I found on clothes at Penney's. And guess who I saw . . . "

And so it goes for the next hour. Janice never mentions one word about the clean rooms. And after her whirlwind entrance the house soon looks like a hurricane had swept through. By now John is doing a slow burn. His anger has reached the boiling point. Is it her behavior that creates John's anger? Or is it his own thoughts? Let's enter his mind to see what he is thinking.

"She should have noticed all this work I did for her."

"She should have thanked me."

"She shouldn't have been so insensitive and inconsiderate."

"What a lousy way to treat me."

"She shouldn't have messed up these rooms."

"Just wait until she wants me to help her! Fat chance."

John's thoughts are making him feel hurt and angry. He *could* have thought:

"I wish she would notice the work I've done."

"Perhaps I did all this for what I would get out of it instead of just helping her."

"I can get along without her noticing. If not, I'll just ask if she noticed anything. I could let her know I have a better understanding of what housework is like."

"Next time I'll find a creative way to let her know her work has been done for her."

This series of thoughts is much more realistic and less emotionally charged. Changing "should" statements to "I wish . . . " or "It would be nice if . . . " will help us use our minds to control our emotions so we can maintain the ability to reason.

Situation 2: Curt was frustrated when he came in for counseling. He was livid with anger at his wife. "You bet I'm angry," he said, "and I've got a right to be. If you had to live with that hypocritical woman you'd be angry too. Oh, she puts on a great performance. She responds with love, kindness, patience, and fairness with everyone else. But at home it's just the opposite! Everyone at church sees her as a saint! Ha! At home she's constantly griping, complaining, running me down, and comparing me to others. If there's a fault to be found with me, she'll find it. She makes life miserable for me and I'm burned up. And don't tell me I don't have a right to be angry. I'm ready to take a walk on her!"

Curt had many expectations for Susan which (from his point of view) were not being fulfilled.

As we talked we discovered that Curt not only had expectations but felt he had a right to demand that she fulfill those expectations. Curt was telling himself that:

1. It is wrong and terrible to be treated by my wife in this way, especially when she demonstrates Christian love to others.

2. I am correct in demanding that she treat me differently than she does.

3. She owes me love and a submissive attitude since she is my wife.

4. She is terrible to treat me this way.

5. She should change her response to me.

Curt's self talk and expectations were creating his anger. As we continued to explore his feelings we discovered that he felt like he was wasting his life with Susan and he wasn't sure that she could change. He believed that (most of the time) he was loving, kind, and considerate with Susan and thus she should respond in like manner.

Curt had three causes for his anger: (1) expectations; (2) a list of shoulds and oughts for Susan; (3) a pattern of self talk which fed his anger.

What Do You Think?

1. If you were counseling Curt what suggestions would you give him for dealing with the above three causes?

2. What new statements would you ask him to make in his mind which would help him with his anger?

The *American Heritage Dictionary* describes anger as a strong, usually temporary displeasure, but does not specify the manner of expressions. You can be just as angry while keeping silent as you can while yelling at someone.

The words *rage* and *fury* are used to describe intense, uncontained, explosive emotion. Fury is thought of as being destructive, but rage can be considered justified by certain circumstances.

Another word for anger is *wrath*—fervid anger that seeks vengeance or punishment. *Resentment* is usually used to signify suppressed anger brought about by a sense of grievance. *Indignation* is a feeling which results when you see the mistreatment of someone or something which is very important to you.

A simple definition of anger is "a strong feeling of irritation or displeasure."

What can you do with your anger? There are several steps you can take to lessen anger and reduce inner tension.

Identify the cause. Your anger is a symptom, the tip of the iceberg. Underlying thoughts or other feelings are creating your sense of irritation.

1. What are your thoughts? Are you applying labels to your spouse? Are you trying to mind read? Are you operating on the basis of "shoulds" or "should nots"?

2. Are you feeling hurt over some situation?

3. Is there something that you are afraid of? Identify your fear.

4. What are you frustrated over? Frustration is one of the biggest causes of anger. If you're frustrated you probably have some unmet needs and expectations—probably unspoken.

Evaluate the reason for your anger. Is your anger directed toward your partner because he did something intentionally and knowingly to hurt or offend you? How do you know it was intentional?

Write out your responses to these questions: How is your anger helpful or useful? Is it going to help you build your relationship or reach the goal that you want?

Apply Nehemiah 5:6-7. In order to reduce your anger you need some practical application of Nehemiah 5:6-7. "Then I was very angry when I had heard their outcry and these words. And I consulted with myself [or thought it over], and contended with the nobles and the rulers and said to them, 'You are exacting usury, each from his brother!' Therefore, I held a great assembly against them."

One way to "consult with yourself" is to make a list of the advantages and disadvantages of feeling and acting in an angry manner. Consider the short-term and long-term consequences of the anger. Look over the list and decide what is the best direction to move.

Another approach is to identify the hot thoughts and replace them with cool thoughts. Hot thoughts are the anger-producing thoughts. David Burns describes a situation in which a couple had disagreements over the husband's daughter from a previous marriage. Sue, the wife, felt that Sandy, the daughter, was a manipulator and led John around by the nose. No matter what Sue suggested he ignored her. As Sue pressured him, John withdrew from her. Sue became more and more upset and angry. Then Sue made a list of her hot thoughts and substituted cool or calm thoughts.

Hot Thoughts	Cool Thoughts
1. How dare he not listen to me!	1. Easily. He's not obliged to do everything my way. Besides he is listening, but he's being defensive because I'm acting so pushy.
2. Sandy lies. She says she's working, but she's not. Then she expects John's help.	2. It's her nature to lie and to be lazy and to use people when it comes to work or school. She hates work. That's her problem.
3. John doesn't have much free time, and if he spends it helping her, I will have to	3. So what. I like being alone. I'm capable of taking care of my kids by myself. I'm

be alone and take care of my kids and myself.

not helpless. I can do it. Maybe he'll want to be with me more if I learn not to get angry all the time.

4. Sandy's taking time away from me.

4. That's true. But I'm a big girl. I can tolerate some time alone. I wouldn't be so upset if he were working with my kids.

5. John's a schmuck. Sandy uses people.

5. He's a big boy. If he wants to help her he can. Stay out of it. It's not my business.

6. I can't stand it!

6. I can. It's only temporary. I've stood worse.[1]

What Do You Think?

1. List some of the hot thoughts you experience.

2. Write out a replacement or cool thought.

3. What do you become angry at the most?

WHAT YOU NEED TO KNOW ABOUT ANGER

The Scriptures teach a balanced perspective on anger. We are to be angry at times, but for the right reasons. We are always to be in control of the intensity and direction of our anger. It is not supposed to dominate us or run out of control. Revenge, bitterness, and resentment are not to be a part of our life. We are to recognize the causes and our responsibility for our anger.

BOTTLED UP OR REPRESSED FEELINGS
ARE LIKE PLUGGING UP A STEAM VENT
OR BOILER.

We are never to deny our anger or repress it, but eliminate it in a healthy manner.

What happens outside of us—external events—do not make us angry. Our thoughts do, whether they are automatic thoughts or ones we choose to think. Realizing that you are responsible for your anger is to your advantage. You have an opportunity to take control of your thoughts and your emotions.

In most situations your anger will work against you and not for you. It can cripple you and make you quite ineffective. Anger can limit your capability to discover creative solutions. If no real solution is available, at least you can free yourself from being dominated by the situation and give up resentment. Can joy, peace, and contentment reside side-by-side with your anger?

If you're angry at your spouse it could be that you believe that he/she is acting in an unfair or unjust manner. By looking at your expectations and beliefs you can lessen your anger. What we label unfair or unjust may be *our* evaluation alone.

Much of your anger may be your way of protecting yourself from what you see as an attack against your self-esteem. If someone criticizes you or disagrees with you or doesn't perform according to your expectations, your self-esteem may be threatened. Why? Because of what others have done? No. Because of your negative thoughts.

You and I have three choices for our anger: (1) we can turn it inward and swallow it, absorbing it like a sponge; (2) we can ventilate it; or (3) we can stop creating it. Let's look first at what happens when we swallow it.

Turning anger inward against yourself can give you hypertension, high blood pressure, ulcerated colitis, or depression. Joseph Cooke describes what happened to him when he internalized his anger.

> Squelching our feelings never pays. In fact, it's rather like plugging up a steam vent in a boiler. When the steam is stopped in one place, it will come out somewhere else. Either that or the whole business will blow up in your face. And bottled-up feelings are just the same. If you bite down on your anger, for

example, it often comes out in another form that is much more difficult to deal with. It changes into sullenness, self-pity, depression, or snide, cutting remarks . . . .

Not only may bottled-up emotions come out sideways in various unpleasant forms; they also may build up pressure until they simply have to burst forth. And when they do, someone is almost bound to get hurt . . . . I remember that for years and years of my . . . life, I worked to bring my emotions under control. Over and over again, as they cropped up, I would master then in my attempt to achieve what looked like a gracious, imperturbable Christian spirit. Eventually, I had nearly everybody fooled, even in a measure my own wife. But it was all a fake. I had a nice-looking outward appearance; but inside, there was almost nothing there . . . .

And way underneath, almost completely beyond the reach of my conscious mind, the mass of feelings lay bottled up. I didn't even know they were there myself, except when their pale ghosts would surface now and then in various kinds of unsanctified attitudes and reactions. But they were there nevertheless. And the time came when the whole works blew up in my face, in an emotional breakdown.

All the things that had been buried so long came out in the open. Frankly, there was no healing, no recovery, no building a new life for me until all those feelings were sorted out, and until I learned to know them for what they were, accept them, and find some way of expressing them honestly and nondestructively.[2]

Bottled-up or repressed anger may emerge in some nondirective ways. When it does, the angry person does not have to admit anger or take responsibility for it. This nondirective expression is usually referred to as passive-aggressive. The person's behavior can manifest itself in several ways. Forgetting is very common: "Are you *sure* you asked me?" or "Are you *sure* that was the time we agreed upon?" If you are the one who asked the question, you begin to wonder and doubt yourself. Actually, you have been set up!

Sarcasm is a "nice" way to be angry. A person is given two messages at one time—a compliment and a put-down. "You look so young I didn't recognize you." "Your new suit is sure radical but I like it."

Being late is another frustrating experience for the one against whom the anger is directed. This behavior may emerge unconsciously—the person is on time to some events but late to others.

Passive-aggressive behavior is unhealthy because: (1) it can become an ingrained pattern of behavior which can last a lifetime; (2) it can distort a person's personality; (3) it can interfere with other relationships.

Another choice is to ventilate all your anger. This may help *you* feel better but the results may not be very positive. And the person on whom you vent your anger certainly won't feel better!

A third choice is to stop creating your anger and/or to control the expression of your anger. How? By changing your thought life.

"Conscious delay" is a procedure which can be used to hold back angry responses or any negative response which has been generated in the mind. It is possible to edit negative thoughts (which is not the same as denying or repressing them) so that you will express yourself or behave in a positive manner. It is not hypocritical nor is it dishonest to edit your thoughts. Ephesians 4:15 states that we are to speak the truth in love. A literal translation of this verse means that we are to speak the truth in such a way that our relationship is cemented together better than before. Totally blunt, let-it-all-hang-out honesty does not build relationships. By editing, you are aware of your thoughts and feelings and you are also controlling them. You are actually taking the energy produced by the anger and converting it into something useful which will build the relationship.

How is it possible to edit my thoughts when I begin to become angry? First of all, make a list of some of the behaviors of your spouse which you respond to with anger.

1. My spouse is usually late, as much as fifteen or twenty minutes. Whenever this happens I become angry.

2. My spouse frequently overspends the monthly household allotment and does not tell me about it.

3. My spouse leaves clothes and dishes around the house consistently and expects others to pick them up.

4. Often when I set up an outing or a date for us (even well in advance) my spouse has already planned something for that time and does not tell me in advance.

What Do You Think?

1. What are some things that make you angry? How do you usually think when these things occur?

2. What is your self talk?

3. What are some of the possible explanations for the way your spouse is behaving?

4. Are you guilty of the same problem or a similar problem? Have you attempted to be constructive and positive in any of your discussions with your spouse about this problem? Will what you are about to say or do reduce the chance of your spouse repeating the same behavior?

5. What are three alternate statements you could make to your spouse to replace your usual response?

Write the above questions on a piece of paper and carry it with you. As you find yourself starting to get angry, take a brief time-out and look at your list.

The Word of God has much to say about anger and uses a number of words to describe the various types of anger. In the Old Testament, the word for anger actually meant "nostril" or "nose." In ancient Hebrew psychology, the nose was thought to be the seat of anger. The phrase "slow to anger" literally means "long of nose." Synonyms used in the Old Testament for anger include *ill-humor* and *rage* (Esth. 1:12), *overflowing rage* and *fury* (Amos 1:11), and *indignation* (Jer. 15:17). Anger is implied in the Old Testament through words such as *revenge, cursing, jealousy, snorting, trembling, shouting, raving,* and *grinding the teeth.*

Several words are used for anger in the New Testament. It is important to note the distinction between these words. Many people have concluded that the Scripture contradicts itself because in one verse we are taught not to be angry and in another we are admonished to "be angry and sin not." Which is correct and which should we follow?

One of the words used most often for anger in the New Testament is *thumas* which describes anger as a turbulent commotion or a boiling agitation of feelings. This type of anger blazes up into a sudden explosion. It is an outburst from inner indignation and is similar to a match which quickly ignites into a blaze but then burns out rapidly. This type of anger is mentioned twenty times (see for example Eph. 4:31 and Gal. 5:20). We are to control this type of anger.

Another type of anger mentioned only three times in the New Testament, and never in a positive sense, is *parorgismos.* This is anger that has been provoked. It is characterized by irritation, exasperation, or embitterment. "Do not ever let your wrath—your exasperation, your fury or indignation—last until the sun goes down" (Eph. 4:26, *AMP*).

"Again I ask, Did Israel not understand?—Did the Jews have no warning that the Gospel was to go forth to the Gentiles, to all the earth? First, there is Moses who says, "I will make you jealous of those who are not a nation; with a foolish nation I will make you angry" (Rom. 10:19, *AMP*).

ACCEPTABLE ANGER

The most common New Testament word for anger is *orge.* It is used forty-five times and means a more settled and long-lasting attitude of anger which is slower in its onset but more enduring. This kind of anger is similar to coals on a barbecue slowly warming up to red and then white hot and holding this temperature until the cooking is done. It often includes revenge.

There are two exceptions where this word is used and revenge is not included in its meaning. In Ephesians 4:26 we are taught to not "let the sun go down on your anger." Mark 3:5 records Jesus as having looked upon the Pharisees "with anger." In these two verses the word means an abiding habit of the mind which is aroused under certain conditions against evil and injustice. This is the type of anger that Christians are encouraged to have—the anger that includes no revenge or rage.

Rage interferes with our growth and our relationships. Rage produces attacks (verbal or physical), tantrums, and revenge. It can destroy other people first and then ourselves.

Resentment is another loser. It breeds bitterness and can create passive-aggressive responses. Resentment can actually destroy us and, in time, other people as well.

Since we are rational creatures we can choose how we will respond to external events. In fact we have more control than we give ourselves credit for. Often, however, our past experiences, memories, and patterns of response tend to hinder us from exercising this control, but we can overcome these influences.

What is indignation and where does it fit into our system of responses? Indignation creates constructive actions to change injustice, to protect ourselves and others.

In his book on anger, Richard Walters compares the effects of all three: rage, resentment, and indignation.

Rage seeks to do wrong, resentment seeks to

hide wrong, indignation seeks to correct wrongs.

Rage and resentment seek to destroy people, indignation seeks to destroy evil.

Rage and resentment seek vengeance, indignation seeks justice.

Rage is guided by selfishness, resentment is guided by cowardice, indignation is guided by mercy.

Rage uses open warfare, resentment is a guerrilla fighter, indignation is an honest and fearless and forceful defender of truth.

Rage defends itself, resentment defends the status quo, indignation defends the other person.

Rage and resentment are forbidden by the Bible, indignation is required.[3]

Rage blows up the bridges people need to reach each other, and resentment sends people scurrying behind barriers to hide from each other and to hurt each other indirectly. Indignation is constructive: it seeks to heal hurts and to bring people together. Its purpose is to rebuild the bridges and pull down the barriers, yet it is like rage and resentment in that the feeling of anger remains.[4]

Dr. Walters' description of the characteristics of indignation is different from rage and resentment in attitudes and purposes. Indignation concentrates on real injustice to other people and/or yourself.

With indignation there is realism. Energy is exerted only if there is a possibility of accomplishment.

Unselfishness is a component of indignation. When we are indignant about something we give or are willing to give, we admit our mistakes and even endure suffering.

An additional element is love. Out of a sense of love and concern for others, indignation arises and is expressed. A person feeling indignation is a person under control. He knows what he is doing and what he wants to express, and his responses are appropriate. Is this the way you respond to your spouse when you are angry? It is difficult to be indignant and not full of rage if we are not endeavoring to live the teachings of Scripture. If there is no fruit of the Spirit in our lives (Gal. 5), what place would indignation find?

Before you express your indignation there are two things you should do: (1) pray about your purpose, your attitude, and your words; (2) write out what you would like to say and visualize yourself saying it.

Before you express your indignation, forgive the other person. Regardless of how the other person responds you then have nothing to lose! Why? Because you are not trying to win!

"Good grief," you say to your spouse. "Anyone with any sense would have brought in the rugs and towels we had airing when he saw a dust storm coming. What's the matter with you, John? Don't you ever think?"

A better way to respond to this anger-producing incident would be to say: "John, you left the rugs and towels out during the dust storm. I'm bothered because it's caused me additional work. I wish next time we have any kind of a storm and I'm not around you would check outside and bring in what might be damaged."

There are four healthy reasons for controlling anger.

The first is that the Word of God tells us to control it. Note the reasons given in these verses.

"Do not be quick in spirit to be angry or vexed, for anger and vexation lodge in the bosom of fools" (Eccles. 7:9, *AMP*).

"He who is slow to anger is better than the mighty, and he who rules his own spirit than he who takes a city" (Prov. 16:32, *AMP*).

"He who has no rule over his own spirit is like a city that is broken down and without walls" (Prov. 25:28, *AMP*).

"The beginning of strife is as when water first trickles [from a crack in a dam]; therefore stop contention before it becomes worse and quarreling breaks out" (Prov. 17:14, *AMP*).

"Good sense makes man restrain his anger, and it is his glory to overlook a transgression or an offense" (Prov. 19:11, *AMP*).

"Cease from anger and forsake wrath; fret not yourself; it tends only to evil-doing" (Ps. 37:8, *AMP*).

"Make no friendships with a man given to anger, and with a

wrathful man do not associate, lest you learn his ways and get yourself into a snare" (Prov. 22:24-25, *AMP*).

These are just a few of the passages.

A second reason is the effect that anger has on our bodies. Our heart rate increases, bowels and stomach tense up, blood pressure increases, lungs work harder, our thinking ability lessens. A continual pattern of anger can make our bodies wear out more quickly. Stifled anger can create irreversible damage.

A third reason concerns the sharing of the gospel. How will others respond to our faith if we are known more for our anger than for our love?

The last reason for avoiding anger is that it interferes with our own growth and development of relationships with others.

WHAT IF MY SPOUSE IS ANGRY AT ME

"My biggest problem," John said as he sat quietly near me, "is that I don't know what to do or how to act when Jean is angry with me. I either withdraw and crawl into a cocoon or I explode viciously. Neither response solves the problem!"

You and I will always live around people who become angry with us. Here are some suggestions for handling their anger.

1. Give the other person permission in your own mind to be angry with you. It is all right. It isn't the end of the world and you can handle it.

2. Do not change your behavior just to keep your spouse from being angry with you. If you do you are allowing yourself to be controlled. If your spouse becomes angry it is his responsibility to deal with it.

3. Do not reward the other person for becoming angry with you. If the person yells, rants and raves, and jumps up and down and you respond by becoming upset or complying with what he/she wants you to do, you are reinforcing his/her behavior. If he/she is angry but reasonable, respond by continuing to state your point in a caring logical manner.

4. Ask the person to respond to you in a reasonable manner. Suggest that your spouse restate his/her original concern, lower his/her voice, and speak to you as though you had just been introduced for the first time.

5. If your spouse is angry you do not have to become angry also. Read back over the Scriptures we listed and apply them to your life.

If anger interferes with your communication, there are ways you can change the pattern.

Identify the cues that contribute to the anger. It is important to determine how and when you express anger. What is it that arouses the anger? What keeps the anger going? What is it that *you* do in creating the anger and keeping it going? Focus only on your part and don't lay any blame on your partner.

One way to accomplish this is by the use of a behavioral diary. Whenever anger occurs each spouse needs to record the following:

1. The circumstances surrounding the anger such as who was there, where it occurred, what triggered it, etc.

2. The specific ways you acted and the statements you made

3. The other person's reactions to your behaviors and statements

4. The manner in which the conflict was evenutally resolved.

Establish ground rules for "fair fighting." (See the chapters on communication for information on ground rules.) Each of you will need to make a firm commitment to follow through in keeping these rules.

Develop a plan of action for interrupting the conflict pattern. This plan should involve immediate action to disengage from the conflict. It should also be a way to face and handle the problem at a later time. Interrupting the conflict is an application of Nehemiah 5:6-7: "I [Nehemiah] was very angry when I had heard their outcry and these words. And I consulted with myself, and contended with the nobles and the rulers."

Even the neutral expression of the phrases, "I'm getting angry," "I'm losing control," "We're starting to fight," "I'm going to write out my feelings," is a positive step. Upon hearing one of these statements, the other spouse could say, "Thank you for telling me. What can I do right now that would help?"

A commitment from both of you not to yell or raise your

voices and not to act out your anger is essential. We call this "suspending" the anger. Agree to return to the issue at a time of less conflict. Most couples are not used to taking the time to admit, scrutinize, and then handle their anger.

The interruption period could be an opportune time for you to focus upon the cause of your anger.

David Mace suggests two more positive ways to control your anger.

> This does not mean you do not have a right to be angry. In an appropriate situation, your anger could be a life-saver. Anger enables us to assert ourselves in situations where we should. Anger exposes anti-social behavior in others. Anger gets wrongs righted. In a loving marriage, however, these measures are not necessary. My wife is not my enemy. She is my best friend; and it does not help either of us if I treat her as an enemy. So I say, "I'm angry with you. But I don't like myself in this condition. I don't want to want to strike you. I'd rather want to stroke you." This renouncing of anger on one side prevents the uprush of retaliatory anger on the other side, and the resulting tendency to drift into what I call the "artillery duel." If I present my state of anger against my wife as a problem I have, she is not motivated to respond angrily. Instead of a challenge to fight, it is an invitation to negotiate.[5]

Ask your partner for help. This step is the clincher. Without it, not much progress can be made. The anger may die down, but that is not enough. Both partners need to find out just why one got mad with the other. If they do not, it could happen again, and again, and again. Your request for help is not likely to be turned down. It is in your partner's best interests to find out what is going on, and correct it if a loving relationship is going to be maintained. When the request for help is accepted, the stimulus that caused the anger is usually completely neutralized and the negative emotion dissolves away. Then the work can begin right away, if possible, or at some agreed upon future time. The whole situation can thus be calmly examined, and some solution found. In fact, conflicts between married people are not really destructive. Rightly used, they provide valuable clues that show us the growing edges of our relationship—the points at which we need to work together to make it richer and deeper.[6]

De-cue your spouse. If you have certain behaviors that tend to provoke anger from your spouse, you should eliminate those behaviors so that your spouse has no reason to retaliate. Minor or even defensive behaviors can be a trigger. Leaving clothes on the floor, a hair dryer on the sink in the bathroom, bringing up the past, banging pots and pans are triggers which are easy to change. If a spouse cowers and this elicits abusiveness, he/she can leave the room before the abuse occurs. In determining the cues it may be important to talk through some of these episodes to discover specific triggers and then to seek alternatives.

Change the faulty thinking pattern that effects the relationship. Here again the problem of expectations and assumptions arises. The faulty beliefs will need to be exposed and challenged. Some common themes are:

"You won't love me if I tell you how I really feel."
"You won't love me if I disagree with you."
"It's better just to hide how I feel."
"It's better just to fake it and go along with what he wants."
"Even if I do speak up, you'll win anyway."
"He should know what I need."
"All anger is wrong so I'm not going to express any."
"I'm not going to lower myself and get angry like he does."

Analyze and challenge the assumptions and eliminate any mind reading.

Redirect your focus from "who is right or wrong?" to "what are the behaviors involved and how do they affect our relationship?"

THE EFFECT OF BLAME

Blame is one of the major cripplers of a relationship. It discourages the healing of hurts and erects even greater walls. When marital discord occurs, each of you usually tries to remove your own guilt. You may look, therefore, for a scapegoat rather than evaluate your own part in the problem. If you can succeed in placing blame, then your own sense of responsibility is lessened. One person attacks, the other person counterattacks. Eventually both become proficient combatants. Each of you struggles under the pain of self-criticism.

Most husbands and wives do not need to refine their blaming skills. Rather, they need to find new ways to avert placing the blame.

There are several practical steps you can take:

1. Instead of blaming or attacking your spouse, share your own inner hurt and feelings. Hurt is usually where the blame is coming from.

2. When you have calmed down sufficiently enough to share complaints in a constructive manner, discuss some of the principles of communication or conflict resolution.

3. It is sometimes difficult, but very necessary, to distinguish between the person and his negative behaviors. This eliminates labeling the person as "bad" or "destructive."

4. If your spouse suggests that you intentionally behaved in a negative manner, you could pose the question, "How would you respond if you knew that what happened was unintentional?" The person's accusation suggests that he is more of an expert on you than he really is. Give him an opportunity to put himself in your shoes.

The Prayer of an Angry Person

Loving God, I praise You for Your wisdom, for Your love, for Your power. Thank You for life, with its joys and mysteries. Thank You for emotions—including anger.

Forgive me when I am led by my anger instead of being led by You. Make me aware of the things I do that produce anger in others—help me change those things. Show me how to clean up the offenses I commit toward others, and give me the courage to ask forgiveness.

Help me to be able to look past the anger of another person and see Your creation in them, and to love them. Teach me how to forgive; and give me the humility to forgive gracefully.

Arouse me to oppose justice and other evils. Show me how to channel my energy that might otherwise be wasted in anger into constructive action in Your service.

You ask me to minister to persons around me. Help me understand what that means. Wake me up. Help me recognize that every moment of my life is an opportunity for Your love to flow through me.

Thank You heavenly Father, for Your love. Thank You for sending Christ so that we might have life and have it to the full, and for sending the Holy Spirit to comfort and guide us through the uncertainties and confusion of everyday living.

In Christ's name, Amen.[7]

What Do You Think?

1. What specific changes do you want to make with your anger?

2. Describe the plan you will implement this week to bring about these changes.

3. Go back through this chapter and list the specific points which will help you the most.

Notes

1. David Burns, M.D., *Feeling Good: The New Mood Therapy* (New York: The New American Library, Inc., 1980), p. 152.
2. Joseph R. Cooke, *Free for the Taking* (Old Tappan, NJ: Fleming H. Revell Company, 1975), pp. 109-110.
3. Richard P. Walters, *Anger, Yours and Mine and What to Do About It* (Grand Rapids: Zondervan Publishing House, 1981), p. 17.
4. Ibid., p. 139.
5. David R. Mace, "Marital Intimacy and the Deadly Love-Anger Cycle," *Journal of Marriage and Family Counseling,* April, 1976, p. 136.
6. Ibid.
7. Walters, *Anger,* pp. 150-151.

CHAPTER 10

MY PARENTS, YOUR PARENTS, AND US

Communication between husband and wife is one thing. But what about communication between you and your parents—yours and your spouse's? And how does your in-law/parent relationship affect your marital communication?

By now you have grasped the importance of past relationships and experiences. The old relationship with your own parents and the new relationship with your in-laws will have a definite effect on your marriage. Positive and healthy relationships with our in-laws and parents are possible. Let's consider some of the areas of potential conflict or harmony.

Each partner brings to the marriage different customs, traditions, and life-styles. In the homes in which we were raised there were housekeeping practices, cooking styles, and family customs which may differ from those of our spouse. We may believe that the way our parents did things was the right way. Christmas holiday customs are a common example. The husband may have been raised in a home where the tree was trimmed the week before Christmas, the presents were opened on Christmas Eve, and a turkey dinner was eaten in early afternoon on Christmas Day. His wife's family may have trimmed the tree on Christmas Eve, opened the gifts the next morning, and sat down to a ham dinner in the evening.

What about those this-is-the-way-we-always-did-it customs that are part of our background and which bring uncomfortable feelings and even conflict if we are asked to change them? Who should compromise? Which family tradition should you adopt? Should a newly married couple always fit into the established family customs of their parents? Or should they begin to develop their own? If you *always* go to your wife's parents' home for Christmas, what would happen if you wanted to go to your parents' or to a friend's home? Do you always have pumpkin pie for Thanksgiving? What happens if you suggest a change? Who makes the gravy for the turkey dinner? And whose recipe is used for the dressing? These sound like small items but they can become major problems if they are part of a family's traditions. Can anyone rationally hold that the practices of one family are "right" and the other's are "wrong"? And how do you communicate to your parents or in-laws that you want to change some customs or start new ones?

One of the major reasons couples come for counseling is because of conflict with their in-laws. There is hurt, bitterness, and misunderstanding. Often one partner feels caught in the middle between his parents and his spouse. Sometimes one or both spouses have not left home psychologically. After marriage, however, a couple's primary allegiance is to each other and not to his or her parents!

There are several factors which can affect the relationship between couples and in-laws.

The ages of the couple in comparison with the ages of the parents are a possible source of conflict. A very young couple who had not made a break from home before marriage by living elsewhere or attending college in another location is faced with this adjustment. At the same time he/she is faced with the adjustment of learning to relate to another person in a marriage relationship.

Most parents of young couples are middle-aged and still involved in their own careers and achievements. They have interests and rewards apart from their married children. If they have assisted their children into adulthood, they may be looking forward to responding to their children now as adults on an equal basis.

But some parents *demand* attention from their children, such as those with a declining income, few outside interests, chronic illness, or very old age. If the parents divorce, their relationship with their grown children may also be affected.

What Do You Think?

1. Are you or your parents in any of these categories? If so, describe the effect it has had on you and your marriage.

2. How have any of these affected your communication?

3. What needs to be done to remedy the situation?

A person's birth order in the family can influence his relationships with his in-laws. If one spouse is the oldest child in a family and the other the youngest, this difference may affect their marriage relationship and also the expectations of their parents and in-laws. The parents of the youngest child may be somewhat reluctant to let go of their last child. The parents of the oldest child may have higher expectations for their son-in-law or daughter-in-law.

What Do You Think?

1. Where are you in the birth order of your family?

2. How is this affecting your marriage?

Couples and parents often have unrealistic expectations of what a relationship should be between themselves. One set of parents may have imagined a close, continuing relationship between themselves and their new son-in-law or daughter-in-law. They assume they will all get together every weekend, call every third day, and enjoy all Thanksgivings and Christmases together. They are also certain that the young couple will never live more than five miles away so they can have constant contact with their grandchildren. And they expect at least four grandchildren, the first within two years!

But what if you have other plans? What if you plan on not having any children, or living 2,000 miles away, and writing your parents once a month? These expectations need to be openly discussed as soon as possible.

What happens when one person comes from a family with close and warm relationships and the other does not? The latter may not want to establish a close relationship with his in-laws. Or the opposite might be true. The person who had little or no warm, close times at home may seek a close relationship with the in-laws. The one whose family was close may want to break away!

A newly married couple's choice of where they live can influence their relationship with in-laws. Couples who live with their parents are only asking for increased conflicts. The young couple will feel restricted in many ways. The wife, particularly, will feel out of place in her mother-in-law's home. When a couple lives with one set of parents, the other in-laws may get jealous and want to do some "controlling" of their own.

What about the life-style and goals of the couple and their parents? Highly affluent, work-oriented parents often have a difficult time restraining themselves from exerting pressure on their married children who may have a different standard of living. The problem is intensified if the couple consistently criticizes their parents' standards.

What differences and similarities do you see in your life-style and goals and those of your parents and in-laws?

And then there is the area of grandparents and grandchildren. Some parents look forward to becoming grandparents and have their own ways of pressuring a couple to "produce." Other grandparents resent being grandparents, it makes them feel old. If a child does not look like the grandparents, is not the sex they were hoping for, or does not behave according to their expectations, conflicts may arise. A frequent complaint in this area is the way grandparents treat their grandchildren when they come for a visit. Some grandparents overindulge or spoil their grandchildren, making discipline that much harder for the parents when the children come back home. And what if the grandchildren prefer one set of grandparents over the other and want to spend time with them and not with the others?

All of these issues affect communication. Perhaps you are struggling with some of these issues right now. Or you may be breathing a sigh of relief and saying, "We're fortunate. We have never had any difficulty." But what will happen when your own children marry. What if problems such as these do occur? What can you do now to prevent these problems from arising when your own children marry and have children?

Here are some typical adjustment difficulties which can occur. How would you communicate with your spouse or your in-laws in order to resolve these problems?

Case 1. A husband judges and criticizes his wife's housekeeping. He keeps referring to how his mother did it and uses her example as a standard. Or a wife continues to refer to her relationship with her own father as a model of what a dad does with children.

Case 2. John's parents constantly criticize him and his wife. They have an opinion for everything, especially how to raise the children. These unsolicited comments are beginning to frazzle John and Betty's nerves. How could they constructively confront John's parents with the problem?

Case 3. Harry's parents are very demanding in a manipulative way. They want attention and have many expectations regarding Harry and Tina's time. When they don't get their way they try to make Harry and Tina feel guilty. Here is a portion of their conversation with Harry. How would you respond to some of these statements?

Mom: Hello, Harry, this is Mom.

Harry: Hi, Mom, how are you doing?

Mom: Oh, all right I guess. (She sighs.)

Harry: Well fine, but how come you're sighing?

Mom: Oh, well, I guess I haven't been doing so well. Anyway are you coming over this weekend? I was hoping to see you. You know it's been several weeks since you and Tina have been over.

Harry: I'm sorry you're not feeling well, Mom. No, we won't be coming over this weekend. We have some other things that we have already planned to do.

Mom: Well, what's more important than seeing your dad and mom? Aren't we important to you anymore? Well, we sure are disappointed. We were positive that you would be over, and I already have a turkey for dinner. Did you know that? You know your brother and sister come over to see us all the time. We don't even have to ask them! A good Christian son wants to see his parents often. If you really loved and cared for us, you would want to come and see us.

Case 4. The husband says: "Every year we have to spend our vacation with my wife's parents. We've done this for the past eight years! And it's not the most relaxing experience either. I feel stuck but what else can we do? They *expect* us to come! I'd like to some some other parts of this country."

Case 5. Another common problem is that of parents who feel they must contact their son or daughter every day. For example, a wife was really bothered because of constant mothering by her mother-in-law. Each day the mother would call and want to know how her son was doing at his job, whether he was gaining or losing weight, eating the right food, whether he had stopped smoking yet, etc. This was a situation in which the mother-in-law needed to stop making the phone calls in order for the wife to feel better. How would you handle the situation?

Here are some possible ways to handle the situations just described.

Case 1. If the wife's cooking (or housekeeping, driving, ironing, etc.) is being compared with her mother-in-law's, she might say something like, "Honey, one of the things I would really appreciate and would make me feel better is for you to let me know when something I've cooked for you pleases you. I do feel hurt when I hear about your mother's cooking all the time. I want to develop my own cooking skills, but I need positive feedback from you."

Or the husband might say, "Honey, I would really appreciate it if you could let me know when I have done something that helps you as you work with the kids. I really become discouraged when I keep hearing about how your dad always did such and such when you were growing up." Both of these statements contain positive and specific comments that are the proper ways to share concern and complaints.

Case 2. This can be a delicate situation which most of us would prefer avoiding. We are afraid of the outcome although we dislike the constant criticism. We are concerned over the potential hurts and anger of our parents if we confront them. Remember that you are confronting them because you care and want a better relationship. If you do not confront them and request a change, in all likelihood your relationship will die. Here are some ways you might confront them.

"I would really appreciate your sharing some positive things about what's going on with you."

"When you have a complaint, I would really appreciate it if you would also suggest something positive that you feel we are doing."

"When we are disciplining the children, I would appreciate your not saying anything about what we are doing in front of them. I am always open to positive suggestions but please share them with me later, when they are not around."

Case 3. Here is the actual entire conversation that Harry had with his mother. This may be a totally different way of responding for you, but Harry's persistence and nondefensive responses were effective.

Mom: Hello, Harry, this is Mom.

Harry: Hi, Mom, how are you doing?

Mom: Oh, all right I guess. (She sighs.)

Harry: Well fine, but how come you're sighing?

Mom: Oh, well, I guess I haven't been doing too good. I don't know what's wrong. Anyway, are you coming over this weekend? I was hoping to see you. You know it's been several weeks since you and Tina have been here.

Harry: I'm sorry you're not feeling too well, Mom. No, we won't be coming over this weekend. We have some other things that we have already planned to do.

Mom: Well, what's more important than seeing your mom and dad? Aren't we important to you anymore?

Harry: I can understand that you want to see us, Mom, and you are important, but we won't be coming over this weekend.

Mom: Well, we're sure disappointed. We were positive that you'd be over, and I already have a turkey for dinner. Did you know that?

Harry: No, Mom, I didn't.

Mom: Both your father and I are disappointed. Here we were expecting you two to come and we have the turkey already bought.

Harry: Mom, I can tell that you're disappointed, but we won't be able to be there this weekend.

Mom: You know your brother and sister come over to see us all the time. We don't even have to ask them!

Harry: That's true, Mom. They do come over more, and I'm sure they're a lot of company. We can plan for another time and work it out in advance.

Mom: A good Christian son wants to see his parents often.

Harry: Does my not coming over make me a bad Christian son?

Mom: If you really loved and cared for us, you would want to come and see us.

Harry: Does my not coming to see you this weekend mean that I don't love you?

Mom: It just seems that if you did, you would be here.

Harry: Mom, not coming over doesn't mean I don't care for both of you. I love you and Dad. But I won't be there this time. I'm sure you can use the turkey now or freeze it. Now, let me check with Tina and look at our schedule and see when we could all get together.

Case 4. Vacations with in-laws can be a problem. One spouse can become irritated and may come away very upset after a lengthy visit. A solution might be to engage in some enjoyable activity elsewhere while his mate visits her own parents alone. This may seem to contradict what people have been taught or what seems to be right. But if the extended stay does not promote better relationships between in-laws and does not have a positive effect upon the marriage, this may be the only solution. I am not suggesting that a spouse never visit his in-laws. But many couples have found the answer to be infrequent visits for brief periods of time.

Another possible solution is to shorten the entire visit. If one person would like to visit his/her parents for a month and the other feels uncomfortable with being there that long, or being separated from his/her spouse for that long, they could compromise. Make the visit for only two weeks. It might also be best not to visit in-laws or parents every year on your vacation. This could create a tradition which you may find difficult to change later on. It also limits your possibilities of enjoying other vacation experiences.

Case 5. Constant contact initiated by the parents may reflect many needs on their part—loneliness, control, a need to be needed, etc. A couple needs to be in agreement as to the approach to take to resolve this particular conflict. They could agree on a goal and then communicate this goal to his mother: "Mom, we do enjoy hearing from you but there really is no need for you to call each day. Why don't we arrange our calls in this way: If we need something or something is wrong we'll be sure to call you. We also would like you to have the opportunity to develop other relationships and not be so dependent on us. You know that you are always invited for dinner on Sunday. Why

TYPICAL ADJUSTMENT DIFFICULTIES

don't you plan to see us on Sundays and call us just on Wednesdays? That way we can stay in touch on a regular basis. In case of emergency you know you can always call."

PRINCIPLES FROM SCRIPTURE

The ideal pattern for any relationship is found within Scripture. In any situation or relationship we need to visualize the Word of God in practice in our lives. Begin by asking yourself, "How do I see myself actually doing what this passage says to do?" Then visualize several practical scenes. If you are going to develop healthy in-law relationships, this process is a must.

What Do You Think?

The Word of God abounds with examples of how we are to live in relation to others. Consider the following passages and apply them to yourself and to your extended family. After each passage write out how you see yourself responding to your in-laws or parents.

1. "Let all bitterness and wrath and anger and clamor and slander be put away from you, along with all malice. And be kind to one another, tenderhearted, forgiving each other, just as God in Christ also has forgiven you" (Eph. 4:31-32).

2. "Pursue peace with all men, and the sanctification without which no one will see the Lord. See to it that no one comes short of the grace of God; that no root of bitterness springing up causes trouble, and by it many be defiled" (Heb. 12:14-15).

3. "Blessed are the peacemakers, for they shall be called sons of God" (Matt. 5:9).

4. "If possible, so far as it depends on you, be at peace with

all men" (Rom. 12:18).

5. "Walk . . . with all humility and gentleness, with patience, showing forbearance to one another in love" (Eph. 4:1-2).

One of the goals of our family relationships is harmony with unity. As people get in the habit of being open, honest, and truthful with one another, deeper relationships develop. But hard work is involved.

Paul wrote, "Make my joy complete by being of the same mind, maintaining the same love, united in spirit, intent on one purpose" (Phil. 2:2). We might define these mandates as follows:

"Being of the same mind"—intellectual unity

"Maintaining the same love"—social unity

"United in spirit"—emotional unity

"Intent on one purpose"—volitional unity

Here are some specific steps you can use to improve your in-law relationships. It is vital that both you and your spouse discuss and apply these together.

Take a positive, optimistic view of your in-law relationships. There are many stereotypes about in-laws, but we need to move beyond these biased perspectives.

Mothers-in-law are not always a curse; often they are a blessing.

Couples do not always find it impossible to live with or near their in-laws; some do so and enjoy it.

Men are not more frequently annoyed by their in-laws than are women. There are actually more conflicts between the husband's wife and his mother!

Keeping quiet about in-law problems is not the best way to deal with them. It is far more preferable to clear up differences as they arise.

A person does not have to feel helpless about his in-law relationships; there is much that can be done to make them satisfactory. We must become willing to take risks, however.

Recognize the importance of your partner's family early in your marriage. Any attempts to ignore in-laws just increases friction.

Evaluate which customs from your family background you want and what new ones you would like to try or to establish. Then communicate these to your parents and in-laws. You may want to change customs every few years. Let parents and in-laws know that you will do this. Remember that as married adults *you* have as much say about what to do on Thanksgiving and Christmas as your parents and in-laws do. Perhaps you have simply not yet exercised your freedom of choice.

Consider the needs of your in-laws at this time in their lives. Often the reason people behave in the way they do is because they are trying to fulfill some particular need. But their behavior may not accurately reflect what their needs really are, and thus we are confused. Have you ever considered that the suggestions coming from your in-laws may reflect some of their own needs? They may not really be attempts on their part to control your lives or interfere.

A young woman shared this experience. Whenever her mother would come over to her home she would constantly check the house for dust and dirt. One day after this woman had worked for hours cleaning the house and scrubbing the floor, her mother came for a visit. As the mother sat in her daughter's kitchen, her eyes spotted a six-inch section of woodwork next to the tile which her daughter had missed. She mentioned this to her daughter. The daughter could feel the anger slowly creeping up through her body and her jaw tensed and her face became red.

Her mother noticed this reaction to her comment and said, "Honey, I can't really be of much help to you in anything else, but this is one thing I can help you with." As she shared, the daughter realized that her own mother felt inadequate and useless around her and this was her only way of attempting to feel useful and needed. Both mother and daughter now have a better understanding of each other.

Most parents-in-law need to feel useful, important, and secure. They still like attention. What could you do to help them fulfill these needs? Have you ever asked your in-laws outright what you could do to help them feel useful? It may take just a few simple actions and the expression of concern on your part to help your in-law feel important and loved.

Treat your in-laws with the same consideration and respect that you give your friends. If your in-laws are Christians, can you see them not just as in-laws but as fellow members of the Body of Christ? Can you see them as brothers or sisters in Christ? If they are not Christians, can you see them as individuals for whom Christ died? Can you remember that God's love is an unconditional commitment to imperfect people? See their potential in the same way God sees them.

When your in-laws show an interest in some area of your life and give advice, respond just as you would if a friend were giving you some advice. If it is good advice, follow it and thank them for their concern. If it is not what you want to do, thank them for their suggestion but continue doing what you had planned to do in the first place.

Some couples say, "But you don't know my in-laws or my parents! They won't give up! They keep on and on, and if one approach doesn't work they will try another, or they will try to divide my spouse and me on the issue!" Perhaps they will, but honest and firm assertiveness on your part will be helpful. They probably continue to press because it has worked for them in the past. If you remain firm and consistent, they will learn that you have the right to respond to their advice and suggestions as just that—advice and suggestions, not absolute laws.

Give your in-laws the benefit of doubt. If they seem overly concerned with your affairs, it could be that they are really concerned with your welfare. They may not be trying to interfere in your life. Could your past experience or self talk be influencing your current response?

Look for positive qualities in your in-laws? Too often we tend to focus on the faults and weaknesses of others and overlook their positive traits.

When you visit your in-laws (and when they visit you), keep the visits reasonably short. Be sure you have plenty to do when you are there. Be as thoughtful, courteous, and helpful as you can be. Consider them as you would your friends. Don't view parents and in-laws as built-in baby-sitters.

Give your in-laws time to adjust to the fact that you are now married. Your mother-in-law has been close to your spouse for many years. Recognize that the process of separation should be as gradual as possible.

If you want to give advice to your in-laws, it is usually best to wait until they ask for it. If you offer a suggestion to them, remember that they have the right to accept or reject it. After all, don't you want the same right?

Don't discuss your disagreements and your spouse's faults with your family. If you do you may bias them against your spouse, thus making it more difficult for all parties involved to achieve a better relationship.

Don't quote your family or hold them up as models to your spouse. He/she will probably feel defensive and seek to defend his/her own parents' ways of doing things, even if you are correct in your statements. If you desire your in-laws to do something differently, ask your spouse how he/she feels about his/her parents. Perhaps he/she can share some insights about their behavior that you cannot see. Remember that both families have their idiosyncrasies and eccentricities. This is called being human!

What Do You Think?

1. What have you done in the past to let both your own parents and your in-laws know they are important to you?

2. During the past two weeks, what have you done to express your positive feelings toward your parents and your in-laws?

3. What additional things could you say or do that would let your parents and in-laws know they are important to you?

4. What have you learned about the kind of relationship your parents or in-laws expect from you and your spouse? (Such as how often to visit or call, their involvement in disciplining your children, etc.)

What should you do about their expectations in the future?

5. In the past, how have you helped your parents or in-laws meet their own needs and develop a greater meaning in life?

How can you help them in the future?

6. If your parents or in-laws have had serious difficulties in the past, how did you respond to them?

How can you be more helpful in the future?

7. In the past, what have you done with your parents or in-laws to make it easier for them to demonstrate love toward you and your immediate family?

How can you improve this in the future?

8. What have you done in the past to assist your parents or in-laws to receive love from you?

What have you done to demonstrate your love to them?

Note

Some material from this chapter has been adapted from *How to Be a Better Than Average In-Law* by Norman Wright (Wheaton, IL: Victor Books, 1981).